Financing Your Franchise

Meg Whittemore

Nation's Business Magazine
Washington, D.C.

Andrew Sherman

Attorney
Washington, D.C.

Ripley Hotch

Editor and Writer
Asheville, N.C.

McGraw-Hill, Inc.

New York   San Francisco   Washington, D.C.   Auckland   Bogotá
Caracas   Lisbon   London   Madrid   Mexico City   Milan
Montreal   New Delhi   San Juan   Singapore
Sydney   Tokyo   Toronto

Library of Congress Cataloging-in-Publication Data

Whittemore, Meg.
    Financing your franchise / Meg Whittemore, Andrew Sherman, Ripley
Hotch.
       p.   cm.
    Includes index.
    ISBN 0-07-056861-8 — ISBN 0-07-056862-6 (pbk.)
    1. Franchises (Retail trade)—United States—Finance.
I. Sherman, Andrew J.   II. Hotch, Ripley.   III. Title.
HF5429. 235. U5W48   1993
658. 8' 708—dc20   93-14238
                                                         CIP

1 2 3 4 5 6 7 8 9 0 DOC/DOC 9 9 8 7 6 5 4 3

ISBN 0-07-056861-8

*The sponsoring editor for this book was David Conti, the editing supervisor
was Joseph Bertuna, and the production supervisor was Pamela A. Pelton. It
was set in Garamond by McGraw-Hill's Professional Book Group composition
unit.*

Printed and bound by R. R. Donnelley & Sons Company.

To the memory of
Raymond J. Whittemore

Contents

Preface

Franchising seems like magic to many would-be business owners. They think of McDonald's, and dreams of independence and wealth dance in their heads. But dreams are not enough; they're only the beginning.

The truth is, franchises are like any other business: lots of work, lots of stress, problems, challenges, terrifying escapes, and, yes, rewards. But nothing is free, and nothing is easy. However, you can make it easier on yourself.

The three biggest decisions in buying a franchise are choosing the franchise, determining the location, and finding the money. Of the three, the hardest is obtaining the necessary financing, and that's the subject of this book.

Of course, we can't really talk about financing without talking about franchising in general, because you need to know what you're up against when it comes to the money. So in Chap. 1, we introduce you to franchising. We begin at the beginning and explain what franchising is and what it is not, how it came to be, and the atmosphere in which it currently operates. Then we discuss how to evaluate your opportunities—how to choose that franchise—and locate it. We also suggest some of the ways you can get into trouble. Only after you have evaluated your opportunities and fitness for franchising do we introduce the particulars of financing. And because financing isn't just a matter of getting money, we also discuss the legal relationships between the franchisee and the franchisor.

Franchising is a matter of knowing who is bringing what to the relationship, and what it might cost you if the relationship goes sour. It's very much to the advantage of both sides for the relationship not to go sour.

Of all the terminology, interestingly enough, the one term most misunderstood is *franchising* itself.

Franchising is a complex subject because it cuts across so many boundaries, and is even now in the midst of changing. Picking your way through the maze of claims made by franchisors isn't easy, but we'll provide the best map we can.

As observers of franchising, we bring a wide range of useful experience to the writing of this book. Each of us has had contact with franchising for some years:

Meg Whittemore entered the franchise arena in 1984 as director of communications for the International Franchise Association (IFA). In October of that year, *Nation's Business* carried her cover story on franchising, kicking off a long-term commitment to franchising coverage by the magazine. In the years that followed, she tracked the growth of franchising in her articles, which appeared in *Forbes, USA Today,* and *INC.,* among others. During a brief stint as an entrepreneur, she counseled franchisors in the areas of marketing and public relations. Now a full-time member of the editorial staff of *Nation's Business,* she regularly covers franchising and small store retailing.

Andrew Sherman's first exposure to franchising was from 1978 to 1982 when he co-founded a Maryland-based sports and entertainment franchise. Since 1986, he has practiced franchise law, focusing on regulatory and corporate finance issues that affect franchisors and franchisees. He has written and lectured extensively on franchising and has authored several books including *One Step Ahead: The Legal Aspects of Business Growth, Franchising and Licensing: Two Ways to Build Your Business,* and *The Franchising Handbook.*

Ripley Hotch began the franchising column for *Nation's Business* in 1985. Since then he has conducted seminars on franchising and has been called upon as an authority on the subject. His previous books include *How to Start a Business and Succeed* and *How to Start and Run Your Own Bed & Breakfast Inn.*

Acknowledgments

We owe thanks to many people who have helped us over the years to understand the franchising phenomenon. We have had the pleasure of watching this business method grow and have been interested observers of its successes and its growing pains.

Our meeting point was *Nation's Business*, the first national business magazine to devote space to a regular column on franchising. That began in 1985.

We have also received help from many individuals and organizations who have served the franchise community: the International Franchise Association, Women in Franchising, U.S. Small Business Administration, the U.S. Department of Commerce's Minority Business Development Agency, the thousands of franchisors and franchisees who have graciously shared their experiences, and the bankers and financial consultants who have generously given us their time and knowledge.

And we would like to acknowledge the assistance of Brent Goldstein in assembling the directory in Appendix B.

Meg Whittemore
Andrew Sherman
Ripley Hotch

1
Introduction to franchising

What is franchising?

One thing we should get clear at the outset: Franchising is not an *industry,* although it is often called one. An industry (or type of business) is categorized by what it makes or by what it provides in terms of service: chemicals, paper, insurance, computers, and so on. Franchising extends across all kinds of industries, although the product of a particular franchise will certainly be within one of them.

Franchising is *a form of distribution or marketing,* nothing more. It is not a particular industry or a way of doing business or a series of voodoo gestures. It isn't a great mystery, although it has come to carry with it a great mystique of inevitable success.

The success rate is impressive. Franchising represents 35 percent of all retail sales in the United States and is expected to climb to 50 percent by the end of the century. Success rates for individual franchisees are equally impressive—the Department of Commerce has placed it at 90 percent, which is far more impressive than the 40 percent success rate for the average small business. Recently Department of Commerce figures have been challenged because they count only franchise locations that were closed, not those that actually failed or those that were forced sales. Our own research indicates that the failure rate of franchises, while still better, is much closer to the average small business start-up than the glowing reports that franchisors would lead you to believe.

Recent hearings before the U.S. House Small Business Committee support these less optimistic figures. The past chairman of the American Bar Association's Forum on Franchising estimates that only one-third of an average chain's franchises does well, another third breaks even, and a third loses money. The consulting firm Rubinoff Rager Inc. estimates that franchise failure rates are about 35 percent, which we believe is a more realistic figure.

This comes as a shock to potential franchisees, but it underlines the need to be wary and to understand what you are getting into.

How franchising began

The first franchises were dealerships. The franchisor owned the trademark for a product, and for a fee produced and distributed the product to the dealer. The dealer was able to offer the product, using the considerable power built up by the franchisor from public recognition of the product. Probably the first franchisor in this country was The Singer Sewing Company, the inventor and peddler of the first automatic sewing machine. The most famous early franchisors were automobile dealers, closely followed by automobile tire makers and soft drink producers. (Yes, Coca-Cola still has franchisees—its bottlers produce Coke under license.)

This kind of franchise—known as a product and trade name franchise—is a territory for the sale of a product. The licensee pays for the privilege, and in return gets (usually) a nationally recognized product to add to its product line. Some of these franchisors are beginning to put more restrictions on the licensee than before—the new Japanese luxury car showrooms are a prime example—but in general the licensee is pretty free to operate as it chooses.

Licensees may introduce additional product lines, display the lines as they wish, or drop lines (all within the limits of the original license agreement, of course). The licensee usually doesn't get training or support (although that has been changing). And there is little to distinguish the franchisee in this kind of business from the entrepreneur who is starting a wholly new business on his or her own.

In the early 1950s, a more complex version of franchising appeared; it has come to be known by the term *business-format franchising*. This is what most people think of when they think of a franchise: fast food, quick printing, tax services, motels, and so on.

What is business-format franchising?

Business-format franchising ties the franchisee very closely to the parent. In the older form, there was nothing to prevent a dealer from having several product lines in its store, and that is still true. A Ford dealer may also carry a Mitsubishi line, a Firestone dealer might carry Michelin, and so on. But a McDonald's franchise never carries Kentucky Fried Chicken.

The business-format franchise is almost always what people think of when they hear *franchising*. This is what we'll mean in the rest of this book. The franchisee in the business-format franchise must do business according to the format laid down by the franchisor.

The contract between the franchisor and the franchisee lays down certain rules for the business relationship. The franchisor agrees to teach the franchisee the format. The franchisor has created a successful, duplicatable format. It works. In return, the franchisee agrees to pay an initial fee and a continuing royalty (a percentage of gross receipts). Sometimes the franchisee buys materials or products from the franchisor, but this is not required; it is against the contract regulations—although some franchisors strongly suggest using certain vendors. Franchisors are not supposed to require franchisees to buy products through them. Usually, franchisees *do* purchase products through the franchisor because of volume discounts.

The advantages to both sides are great. The franchisee gains a workable, tested business format that considerably reduces the risks involved in starting a new business. The franchisor avoids the considerable risks of putting up its own money for every outlet of the business. However, there are also limits imposed by the relationship.

Business-format franchising prescribes how the business will be run, right down to color choices, signage, location, and so on. There's a very good reason for this: The franchisee wants the advantage of national marketing created by the franchise chain because there are many of the same kind of buildings and products out there. When a franchise is done properly, consumers who are seeking to buy a particular product with which they are familiar can find that product no matter where they might be. The franchisor does not want the franchisee to experiment because that would present a different face to the public, causing confusion and loss of business. Franchising is not the place for originality at the outlet level.

Franchises exist because America has a large and mobile population that likes to find a familiar store. People are reassured by the familiarity of the franchises they have come to know. You recognize McDonald's or Burger King or Jiffy Lube wherever you go. The signage is the same, the way the franchise works is the same, even the prices are very close.

If a particular franchisee decides it wants, say, a green sign instead of a red one, it loses the advantage created by all those other red signs in the country, and it contributes nothing to the identity of the business.

The parent company will be very particular about having its format followed. Franchisees who stray, unless they introduce a useful innovation that can be adopted systemwide, are liable to disciplinary action up to and including the loss of the franchise. For this reason, you need to be the kind of person who likes to color within the lines. If you are independent and want to do things your own way, you might be a first-rate entrepreneur, but you won't be a good franchisee.

How does a franchise work?

As a franchisee, you purchase a franchise area and pay a fee, ranging from a few thousand dollars to several hundred thousand, for the right to operate a franchised outlet. That fee will not include certain other costs, such as alterations, rent, purchase of equipment and supplies, signage, and all the other investments that go into opening a new business.

In exchange for the franchise fee, the franchisor gives you exclusive right to your territory and trains you in the business format and procedures to operate the outlet. The franchisor also offers help in site location, marketing, opening promotions, and continuing help and advice as you begin your operation. The franchisor also should offer discounts on products you might need (although it cannot require you to buy products), and should offer all kinds of product improvements as they are developed.

In return, you as the franchisee agree to pay the franchisor a regular percentage of gross sales as a royalty (it ranges from 3 percent to 7 percent, sometimes more) and another percentage as an advertising fee (usually 1 percent to 3 percent), and you agree to operate according to the format outlined by the franchisor.

The advantages to both sides should be clear: The franchisee gets a lot of help, and the franchisor gets an income stream from the royalties.

It's a particularly close and occasionally confining relationship. If it works well, you have a senior partner who warns you of what the market is doing, monitors your outlet to make sure you are operating as you should, and offers you the marketing power of national recognition.

In return, you give up a good part of the freedom of owning your own business. You cannot simply decide that you are going to change the colors of your sign from red and white to blue and orange. That would be grounds for the franchisor to revoke your license. Any franchise contract will list reasons for lifting a franchise before the term of the license is out, so you need to pay attention to those terms.

There are a couple of variations on standard franchising that are worth mentioning here. You may not be dealing directly with the franchisor if that franchisor has sold an *area* or *master franchise*. That gives the franchisee exclusive rights to expand within a given region, with the franchisee deciding how many units there will be. This master franchise can then sell *subfranchises* in that area, and you might be such a subfranchisee.

You may not be able to tell the difference, but you should be aware of the limits of the subfranchisee's rights and responsibilities. You'll need to exercise care in examining the disclosure documents, and we'll go into this in Chaps. 3 and 9.

What can be franchised?

The product of a franchised outlet must support not just one business, the outlet, but *two* businesses, the outlet and the parent company. For that reason, cost controls and efficiency have to be exceptionally high. Good franchises require a lot of discipline.

They also have to add perceived value to a popular product. It isn't enough to copy someone else's formula; something has to be different about it. Much more important is that the product has to be inexpensive to produce: pizza, lubrication service, sandwiches, for example.

The product or service has to be something that can be standardized and controlled. Specialty stores with high-end products simply don't lend themselves to the kind of volume and added value that make them successful as franchises.

Computers have made it possible for office services to be franchised with the same added value as pizza. Accounting services have been successfully franchised. So have mail services, because the U.S. Postal Service is unable to provide the same level of service at the same price and the convenience of location that a Mail Boxes Etc. can.

Housekeeping services, which were a cottage industry before, have been franchised because the franchisors have been able to standardize cleaning methodology, creating teams of cleaners who move methodically through a residence or office, cleaning in a tenth of the time as a traditional cleaning person.

In the case of service, you, as a franchisee, have to be able to multiply yourself; it's usually not productive to do all the work yourself. In order to make a good living, you would have to charge high rates for a unique service. Neither of these is typical of a franchise.

Marketing, discipline, method, volume, cost control—these are the factors that make a successful franchise. In looking at a franchise, and considering the financing, keep all these factors in mind.

The recent history

When business-format franchising was introduced by McDonald's and Holiday Inn, its success was phenomenal. Of course, it helped that the 1950s was a period of rapid economic growth backed by a rapidly growing population that was on the move. Dozens of franchises popped up, and the franchising of America was on its way.

This was a new business form, created by opportunity, ingenuity, and unusual historic circumstances. Most Americans thought of business as big business; the entrepreneurial small business boom was still 30 years away. Most people did not know how to start a business of their own. The idea was scary, and there were few road maps.

Business-format franchising provided a road map. You weren't entirely alone in starting the business or in running it. You could buy into something successful at the start.

Many made fortunes, especially those who bought area franchises—the license for an entire state or region—for the most popular companies. As a new form, however, franchising also attracted some unscrupulous operators who saw a chance to prey on would-be business owners with little knowledge and less experience.

There were several major abuses: promising high profits that were untrue (called *earnings claims*), not delivering support contracted for, taking franchises back without just cause, and not having enough capital to continue the parent company. Franchisees plunked down their life savings for a chance at independence, only to find their business gone, their nest egg gone, and no one even to sue.

As a result of these abuses, the Federal Trade Commission (FTC) stepped in to provide some safeguards in the form of a Franchise Disclosure Rule, governing the definition of franchises and what franchisors can legally say to the potential franchisee.

The FTC rule sets up several definitions for the franchise business: it has to license a trademark to its franchisees, it must charge a fee of $500 for the initial licensing, and it must exercise significant control over the way the franchisee operates the business.

A number of sharp operators sell "licenses" for businesses that look very much like franchises, but they have only a $495 licensing fee. Because that fee is below the cutoff of $500 for initial franchise licensing, these operations are not subject to the FTC rule. Beware of these "business opportunities." Too many people have been burned by them.

Any business that meets the three requirements of trademark, $500 licensing fee, and significant control over format is subject to federal franchise laws. Those laws regulate what a franchisor may and must tell the potential franchisee, to be included in the Uniform Franchise Offering Circular.

A number of states—but not all—have additional franchise regulations. The toughest are in New York and California, and franchisors that are properly licensed in those states are certain to have met more stringent requirements (more on legal issues in Chap. 3). Still, regulations in general are fairly loose, and some abuses still continue. Particularly notorious are versions of earnings claims that ride the coattails of the generally rosy picture the franchise community paints of franchisee success.

In fact, the same abuses are prompting a close look by the U.S. Congress at franchise operations. For example, Movieland U.S.A., a recent franchisor in the notoriously difficult video rental business, sold franchises at $125,000 a pop, only to fold, sinking the trusting franchisees who bought into the business.

The areas most troubling to those considering more regulation for franchising are the kinds of information franchisors must disclose to potential franchisees and the relationship between franchisors and franchisees when the business is up and running. In Chap. 2, we'll look in detail at what disclosure is required—and what you should expect.

New measures being proposed in Congress would require franchisors to exercise good faith and due care in dealings with franchisees, as well as prevent them from terminating franchises without "good cause." The proposed laws would require franchisors to disclose projected costs and probable profits before the sale of the franchise. The laws would also prohibit fraud and deceptive practices in franchise relationships.

Franchisors are not particularly happy about these proposed regulations because they could open the way for a large number of federal lawsuits. What it will probably mean in the long run is that franchisors will be even more careful in choosing their franchisees.

Recent legislation in Iowa is being looked at with interest because it strengthens the rights of franchisees. It requires franchisors to guarantee exclusive territories to franchisees. Legislation of this kind will help put unscrupulous franchisors on notice. It won't stop them, however. And winning a lawsuit against a bankrupt franchisor will only assuage your pride, not your bank account. The best assurance of a successful franchise is for you to undertake a thorough investigation before you put your money down—or go looking for it.

The future

Predictions about franchising's future remain rosy. Franchising is such a useful way of getting a product or service to the general public, and it generates such a strong repeat and referral business that it is bound to be helpful to anyone who wants a business of his or her own.

In the mid 1980s, the Naisbitt Group, headed by John Naisbitt (who wrote *Megatrends*) did a study for the International Franchise Association (IFA) that predicted franchising would continue to grow strongly. The IFA estimates that franchising will account for more than half of all retail sales in the United States by the end of the century.

There are now more than 500,000 franchisees in the country, and one is added every 15 minutes. Sales growth averaged 10 percent a year in the late 1980s and early 1990s, far faster than the economy as a whole.

What are the best franchises?

This is usually the first question anyone who is interested in franchising asks. Everyone wants to be in on the next McDonald's, and franchisors often compare themselves to the most famous of franchises.

The possibilities are extremely varied. The "best" franchise is not always the most obvious. There are many kinds of franchises that you may not even have thought of which might be perfect for you. In the next chapter we'll go into how you can decide what franchise is best for you, but for now we'll go into some trends of the last decade of the century that suggest where the next McDonald's might be.

The Naisbitt study listed the top 10 franchise industries as these: restaurants; retailing other than food; hotels, motels, and campgrounds; convenience stores; business aids and services; automotive products and services; retailing (food other than convenience stores); rental services; construction and home services; recreation, entertainment, and travel (see Fig. 1-1).

Of these, some are more mature than others. In the cost-conscious 1990s, faster growth will probably come in services and products that save money. Fast food will always be strong, but there is a real danger of faddishness. The most open area is probably ethnic foods, healthier foods (that still have taste), and specialty foods.

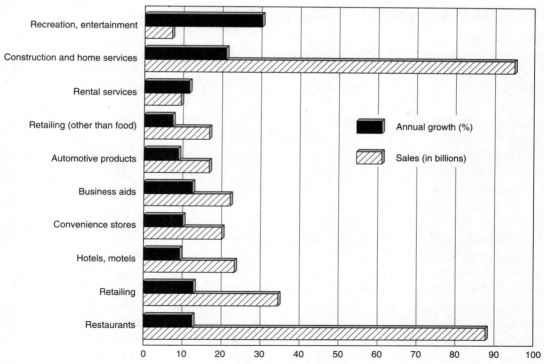

Fig. 1-1 Top franchise industries. (*Internation Franchise Assn.*)

Business services will also continue to be very strong as more people start businesses of their own—franchised or otherwise.

Family is growing in importance for Americans, so anything that promotes family time will be appealing. Travel services that cater to families will be strong. The hotel/motel industry, however, is overbuilt, and only the best locations will be worth considering.

Remodeling and repairs will be strong as well, as many people decide to fix up rather than buy up.

Franchises that are in very narrow niches will have trouble if their niche is easy to copy. We'll talk more in the next chapter about how to make sure you avoid getting into too competitive a field.

A strong trend in franchising is international, if you're willing to consider going overseas. Other countries are as interested in franchised businesses as the United States; the Japanese even think that Seven-Eleven is a Japanese company!

Your job now is to match your means and abilities with a franchise. The right match is important before you even begin to look for the money.

Franchising responds to the market

You probably should engrave those words on your forehead so that you will remember that franchising is a marketing method. Because it is, you have several balls to keep in the air at once. One is the product: Is it something that people are going to want for the foreseeable future, or is it going to have to change? Another is the method that will bring in clients: Will your franchise company be quick to change and improve its marketing methods to appeal to a changing market?

People are changing, as they always have. But the challenge facing franchisees and potential franchisees was clearly underlined in the 1992 election. Bill Clinton is the first baby-boomer president, and he got to the White House using unheard-of and often shocking (to an older generation) means to put his candidacy across, from appearing on talk shows to playing the saxophone on *The Arsenio Hall Show*. Clinton's generation is going to be one of the largest markets for franchises.

Barbara Hollis and Aaron Shingler of Shingler-Hollis Investment Group in Lanham, Maryland, have been looking at franchising trends for a number of years. They have identified several important groups that will have a major impact on franchising as well as all businesses:

- Baby boomers
- People who are over 50
- Women
- Minorities

Baby boomers are now in the seats of power, but they're not always happy. They are growing more conservative, so they keep their cars and homes longer. That means they will have some money left over for the kinds of luxury purchases the generation has become known for.

But because homes and cars will be getting older, boomers will be looking for all kinds of repair and maintenance services for these two major items. The automotive aftermarket will be strong, as will cleaning and baby- (and pet-) sitting services.

The older generation (50+) is another huge number. Just as in Japan, the population in the United States is aging. People live longer and better, and they take better care of themselves. After retirement (or semiretirement) they often continue to work; therefore, they have more income to spend as they choose. But an important chunk of their income goes to health care. So franchises that are in the health care field will have some real opportunities. The greatest success opportunities will come in those franchises that are good at controlling the runaway cost of health care—ambulatory care clinics, for example, that handle routine health problems at a minimum cost by using paramedics.

Women in the work force are not able to do the kind of home care that their mothers did. They bring in more money, but often feel stretched in cleaning, cooking, decorating, and other chores that used to fall to women in the home. Fast food franchises have done well as more people eat out. House cleaning and repair and maintenance franchises will have opportunities because of this trend. Women who work will be tired and will want to spend as much time as they can with their families rather than mopping the floor.

Minorities, particularly Hispanic and Asian minorities, are growing rapidly in this country. Many franchises will be sold to minorities, who in turn will help sensitize their franchisors to the requirements and opportunities of serving these specialized audiences.

This also points to another important trend that is driving the direct marketing industry: It is no longer easy to find a mass market. As markets continue to fragment—everyone wants to be different these days—franchise systems will have to find ways to appeal to them. One way is that franchisors are creating subsidiary franchise chains that are close to, but not exactly like, their main line. Stores of this kind will have widely spaced locations, but can be very profitable. The flip side is that such chains will necessarily grow slowly and will not have the same kind of instant national recognition afforded the McDonald's of this world.

One trend that cuts across all demographic lines—almost a drumbeat theme of the 1990s—is the desire to create your own business. You, after all, are interested in that. So are baby boomers, women, minorities, and even retirees. That means there will be a demand for services that make a start-up business seem like a big one, and we expect the business services field to be one of the fastest growing of the decade.

2

Evaluating franchise opportunities

Although a good franchisor and a good product will generally make for a happy franchisee, you have to do the work to find the right franchise for yourself. Only you know what the match should be and with what you feel comfortable.

In some ways, the relationship between franchisor and franchisee requires more trust than can easily be managed over long distances. The franchisee gives over considerable financial resources to the franchisor in exchange for a business format, exclusive territory (usually), and continuing support. The franchisor provides that in exchange for a franchise fee and monthly royalty. Much of what passes for execution of the contract on both sides is subject to interpretation. Careful investigation and a thorough understanding of the contract is the best way to ensure that not too much is left to interpretation.

In order to make your choice, you need to make some judgments about yourself, what interests you, what your financial resources are, what franchises might be available to you, the advantages of those franchises, the quality of the franchisor (including support policies), and the probable future market value of the franchise.

This is a difficult, sometimes exhausting, task. But you are talking about a major part of your future, and of your resources, so it is essential for your security and peace of mind that you be as painstaking about this evaluation as you can.

The trouble is that all these things intertwine so that as soon as you get one clear in your mind, a shift somewhere else changes your landscape of opportunity. The place to begin, therefore, is where there will be little change.

You

In the last chapter we suggested that the nature of franchising means that some kinds of people make happier—and therefore generally better—franchisees.

There are two areas of self-evaluation that you need to undertake. One is "hard"—financial facts about your resources and your abilities. The other is "soft"—the kind of person you are, and how you might fit with a given franchise.

Begin by filling out the forms presented in Figs. 2-1 and 2-2. They will give you some yardsticks when the sales hype gets heavy.

Franchisors will expect you to fill out a financial sheet for them as well, so it is good to have the information handy. Some are quite up-front about what they expect—one large fast food franchisor, for example, says that all you need is a net worth of $250,000, with $100,000 of liquid assets to get started.

If you find yourself with a negative net worth, you'd better keep working at your day job until your finances turn around.

Assets
 Nonliquid:
  Principal residence _____
  Other real estate _____
  Vehicles _____
  Personal property (furnishings) _____
 Liquid:
  Checking _____
  Savings _____
  Stocks and bonds _____
  Insurance _____
  Spouse's income _____
   (if one of you will
   continue to work) _____
Total assets _____
Liabilities
 Mortgage _____
 Credit card balances _____
 Outstanding loan balances _____
  (car, student, etc.)
Total liabilities _____
Net worth (subtract liabilities from assets) _____

Fig. 2-1   Financial fact sheet.

Circle any that apply; be honest with yourself.

1. Is your health
    a. poor?
    b. fair?
    c. good?
    d. excellent?
2. At what point in a week do you grow tired of working at one thing?
    a. 40 hours
    b. 50 hours
    c. 60 hours
    d. 70 hours
3. I like to
    a. work with numbers.
    b. keep everything orderly.
    c. make sure details are right.
    d. have a clear plan to follow.
4. I don't like to
    a. take orders.
    b. plan activities.
    c. spend time in meetings.
    d. work by myself.
5. When it comes to people, I like to
    a. give written orders to my staff.
    b. have several assistants to disseminate orders.
    c. work with a team.
    d. deal with customers.
6. My family is
    a. indifferent to my franchising idea.
    b. willing to consider helping.
    c. curious and interested.
    d. enthusiastic about getting involved.

Scoring: Give yourself 1 point for each "a" answer, 2 for each "b," 3 for each "c," and 4 for each "d." If you score less than 10, you may be better suited as an independent entrepreneur. If you score between 10 and 16, you'll have to work pretty hard at being a franchisee. A score above 16 indicates that you'll make a good franchise.

Fig. 2-2   Personal fact sheet.

Do you have the personality?

It's important that you feel you are going to be spending your time in a way that is satisfying. It's safe to say that not everyone is suited for a franchise. If you aren't the right type of person, don't let it bother you. It's better to know now, before you waste your money and your time.

The inventory in Fig. 2-2 is brief, but it will help you get a sense of those intangibles that directly affect your chance of success in a franchise outlet. Use these questions to jog your thinking; try not to "weasel" around any of them. In the long run, you'll be better off if you're honest. If you are going into this with a spouse or partner, then both of you need to fill out the inventory separately, then compare notes.

How to find franchises

A number of publishers are finding it lucrative to put out lists of franchises, sometimes with rating systems that suggest the better ones. Some publications are more thorough in specific areas. Others simply list everyone. Some sell the listings to franchisors. Others actively seek out franchise listings and attempt to make them complete. Still others wait for the franchisors to come to them.

It's like everything else in this world; nothing can be all things to all people. Therefore, we recommend that you gather up a number of the following publications (you may find some that we haven't noted). Then compare the listings in the various publications to see what is highlighted.

The International Franchise Association. This is an organization of franchisors that is committed to ethical practices. It publishes a magazine and several guides to franchising. Contact the IFA at 1350 New York Ave., NW, Suite 900, Washington, DC 20005-4709.

The Franchise Annual. This is a good guide to specific franchises. It is published by Info Press, 728 Center St., P.O. Box 550, Lewiston, NY 14092; (716) 754-4669.

The Encyclopedia of Franchises. This book, by Dennis L. Foster, is published by Facts on File, 460 Park Ave. South, New York, NY 10016.

Franchises You Can Run from Home. This book, by Lynie Arden, is published by John Wiley & Sons, 605 Third Ave., New York, NY 10158.

Franchise Opportunities Guide. This is one of the publications from the International Franchise Association, 1350 New York Ave., NW, Suite 900, Washington, DC 20005-4709.

Several magazines, including *Nation's Business, INC., Entrepreneur,* and *Success,* have advertising from franchisors. These ads will often mention the startup costs for a franchise.

Make a list of franchise possibilities based on this first research. All of the publications give you some advice about franchising in general and how to use their listings. If, in making your lists, you find that you have only one franchise in a given category—say office services, or pizza, or hair care, go back and include at least one competitor in each of your interest fields. Then write to the franchisors and request their sales packet; if you get no response, either the franchisor is not reputable or it isn't interested in new franchisees. Find another in that category.

3

"Red flags" in evaluating a franchise

By now you have a good understanding of what franchising is and how it started in this country. You may even be at the point of deciding what kind of franchise business you might like to own and operate.

As with any other purchase that brings you closer to realizing a dream, buying a franchise carries with it a certain excitement—some franchisees have described it as an "emotional high." Making an "emotional" buy when shopping for a franchise is a very dangerous thing. Because the price tag to own a franchise is often hundreds of thousands of dollars, now is not the time to be carried away with the excitement of the moment.

We have talked with thousands of franchisees over the years, and they have shared their successes—and failures—with us. The most tragic failures occurred when franchise buyers "lost their heads" over the thought of owning a franchise and made their purchase too quickly. The result was that they often ended up losing the franchise and everything else they had too.

Successful franchisees strongly advise you to replace your *excitement* over buying a franchise with some hard-nosed *logic* about making such a purchase.

So the first "red flag" to be aware of is yourself—or, more specifically, your emotions. Evaluate why you are making the decision to buy a certain franchise. The best way to ensure that the franchise purchase you are considering is a good one is to take the *time* to investigate the parent company. In Chap. 2 we talked about the kinds of things to consider as you research the possibility of franchising. In this chapter we tell you about the trapdoors to look out for along the way.

The slick sales presentation

Every franchise company has a sales and marketing department. Sometimes it's the franchisor and sometimes it is a full-time marketing professional on staff. These are the people you talk to initially, either by telephone or face-to-face at a regional trade show. Their job is to sell franchises.

A good sales and marketing person will assume that you do not know anything about the franchise and proceed to give you as much information as they can to help you decide if you might be interested in their business. They should also ask you questions about yourself, your experience, and your goals. Franchisors have a reputation to protect, and they should be as interested in learning about you as you are in learning about them.

So the second word of caution is to watch out for a franchise operation that isn't interested in you, your background, the skills you bring to the partnership, your personal goals, family support, and so on. If the only question asked of you is whether or not you can afford to buy the franchise, walk away. The company is selling to you instead of inspecting you, and that's a bad sign.

Franchising carries with it a degree of risk. Depending on the franchise, the risk is sometimes quite high. There are enough documented stories about people who invested their retirement savings, leveraged their homes, and cashed in their life savings and then lost it all because they didn't clearly understand the full range of the risk they were embracing.

Franchisors have a responsibility to make sure that you know and understand the risk you are about to take. They are risking something too. If you fail, they lose an income stream. Their loss, however, is not as potentially devastating as yours, because presumably you are not their only franchisee.

Therefore, another red flag should go up if the franchise sales representative does not acknowledge the risk involved in franchising or will not tell you how the franchisor intends to minimize that risk for you.

Another area to examine carefully is what is involved if you decide to get out of the franchise? Does the company have a policy that requires you to pay them to leave? If the answer is yes, then the franchise company has an incentive to see you fail—not a good sign for a happy long-term relationship.

Lawsuits

A franchise company may be sued for a variety of reasons and the circumstances surrounding a lawsuit may be as numerous. Watch out for any franchisor who tries to hide from or gloss over the details of any lawsuits filed against the company.

By law, a franchisor is required to list all past and current lawsuits that have been filed against the company. The information is contained in the franchise offering circular, which is what the prospective franchisee receives prior to making the final purchase. Be sure to read this section carefully. Excessive lawsuits against the franchisor could mean that there may be trouble for you down the road.

Under the law, franchisors are only required to report litigation that has to do with deceit, fraud, or situations in which money or property were allegedly stolen.

When reviewing information about a franchisor's litigation cases, look at the reasons cited in the individual lawsuits. If you see a pattern forming, take heed. This should be an area that you discuss thoroughly with the franchisor. Sometimes, if a franchise company has changed ownership, the new management has taken steps to correct the problems that caused the lawsuits. If that is the case, the franchisor should be very open and willing to share that information with you.

If the franchisor is reluctant to discuss the litigation cases filed against the company, then you should be wary. This could mean that the franchisor is hiding something that could have an impact on your long-term chances of success. At the very least, hesitation to fully discuss any part of the lawsuits is an indication of the franchisor's reluctance to clearly communicate with you.

A final word: Just because a franchisor has been sued doesn't necessarily mean you shouldn't consider buying a franchise. It *does* mean that you should be on your guard and satisfy every question you have concerning the background of the lawsuits, the status of them, and what the franchisor is doing to rectify the problems raised by the litigation.

Disgruntled franchisees

Part of the process of researching a franchise is to talk with as many franchisees in the system as possible. The franchise disclosure document contains a complete list of the franchisees in the system. Be wary if you are presented with a list of franchisees to contact that are hand-picked by the franchisor.

Every company will have some franchisees who are dissatisfied with one or more aspects of the business. Even though franchising enhances your chance of success, a lot still depends on what an individual brings to the partnership. Some disgruntled franchisees may be voicing their discontentment over their own abilities, a weak economy, or poor sales because they didn't make a strong enough effort—none of which reflect on the franchisor's level of support or training.

Keep in mind that the kind of complaints you are looking for are ones that directly point to the franchisor's lack of training, support, or follow-through. As you do your research, if you hear a number of similar complaints from franchisees, it could mean that there is a serious communication problem—or worse—with the franchisor. If the franchisor denies the existence of the problem, then a red flag should go up.

Check out the level of franchisee turnover. If you see a high or moderate turnover rate—franchisees leaving the system before their 10-year contract is expired—ask the franchisor some questions about the reasons behind the departures. Be cautious if you can't get answers if the franchisor tries to avoid the discussion.

If possible, get a list of the franchisees who left. Many franchisors will give you such a list upon request. Franchisees leave the system for a variety of reasons, and a high departure rate doesn't always mean there is trouble. Sometimes new franchisees discover they just didn't like running a small business. Others, however, may have been encouraged to leave because they couldn't produce a high enough sales volume to produce a profit. You need to know the reasons behind the departures. It could save you from a similar fate.

Earnings claims

Franchisors are not allowed by law to predict what you might earn as a franchisee in their system. They *can* share the profitability of the franchise company–owned stores, but that information must be in writing and it is usually found in the franchise offering circular.

Under no circumstances is a franchisor allowed to *verbally* make earnings projections to you. (See item 7 in the section entitled "Ten trapdoors" on page 30). If an earnings claims discussion starts at a trade show, for example, you are either dealing with an unscrupulous franchisor or a business opportunity enterprise. (Business opportunities often masquerade as franchises, but they are not regulated. You proceed at your own risk.)

Typically, franchisors are extremely careful not to discuss earnings potential. Nevertheless, it is wise to be aware of the restrictions in the earning claim area since promises of "get rich quick" sometimes encourage the buyer to make a hasty decision.

Weak financial statements

A company's financial statement is a snapshot of its overall health. One of the things to look out for when reviewing a financial statement is how heavily the franchisor depends on the royalty stream from the franchisees.

Do the company-owned stores provide the bulk of support for the parent company? They should. If you see a pattern of overdependence on the royalty stream it could mean that the entire franchise system is on shaky financial ground.

It is a good idea to have an accountant or a franchise lawyer look at the financial statements of the franchise you are considering. Also, when talking with other franchisees, try to get an idea of how *they* perceive the financial strength of the franchise.

Unprotected trademarks

Unprotected trademarks is a serious area of consideration because the trademark of the franchise is part of what you are buying when you pay the franchise fee. If the company does not have a protected trademark, your investment in the business is unprotected too.

An unprotected trademark means that your competition can mimic your product, service, signage, and overall business, thus undercutting your market presence. A lawyer should be able to determine if the company's trademark has been filed properly.

Corporate store ownership

As you gather information on a franchise, you will notice that a number of the franchises within the system are owned by the company. This is good because it means the company believes in its own product and service enough to own and operate its own franchises. It also means that the company has tested the franchise methodology before you buy into the system.

What you are looking for when considering a franchise are patterns of corporate store ownership. Does the company arbitrarily open a store close to a successful franchisee's location? If the answer is yes, it could mean that the company-owned location drains the customer base from the franchisee—a situation known as cannibalization of the profit stream.

Another pattern to watch out for is whether the franchisor "buys out" franchisees, only to turn around and sell the same location to another buyer. This is called *churning*—the franchise company buys out a failing franchise at below-market prices and collects another franchise fee from the new buyer.

Investigation into allegations of churning and cannabilization has been conducted by the U.S. House Small Business Committee. Legislation aimed at curbing inappropriate behavior from the franchisor is before the U.S. Congress.

Ten trapdoors

Franchise companies will always present you with their best side, and usually that is an accurate picture. Still, there are areas to watch out for, as we have discussed.

We have compiled a list of 10 items that are absolute sure-fire reasons to walk away from a deal. Here they are.

1. *Franchisors who insist that you don't need to read their franchise disclosure document.* According to a study done by the Federal Trade Commission (FTC), about 40 percent of new franchisees sign a franchise agreement without reading it.

2. *Franchisors who tell you not to bother with having a lawyer or an accountant look at the disclosure document.* The franchise disclosure document is very detailed. It is in your own best interest to hire a reputable attorney who knows franchise law.

3. *A franchisor who doesn't give you a copy of the disclosure document at your first face-to-face meeting to discuss the franchise.* Federal fines of up to $10,000 are levied for each violation of this procedure. Report violations immediately to the Bureau of Consumer Protection at the FTC.

4. *A franchisor who pressures you to sign the franchise agreement before the legally required 10-day waiting period.*

5. *Thin management.* A management team is "thin" if it is inexperienced in franchising or if there is an overly strong dependence on one member of the team. Make sure you are going to get the support you are paying for. Check to see how many supervisors there are in the system.

6. *A marginally successful prototype store or no prototype at all.* Often this means that the franchisability of the product or service is untested. If you buy a franchise with no track record, you sometimes become the guinea pig.

7. *A franchisor who makes verbal projections about how much you can earn.* Any projections have to be made based on what the franchisor is making in the company-owned stores. If the projections are based on what franchisees have made, then those earnings must be put in writing and are legally required to be disclosed in most states. If franchisors don't put earnings projections in writing and just tell you orally, it is a violation of federal law.

8. *A franchisor who has no operations manual or a shallow one.* The idea behind franchising is for you to minimize the mistakes in starting a business. You do that by following the tested methodology set forth by the franchisor in a manual. If there's no manual to follow, you could be headed for trouble.

9. *A franchisor who offers either a very short or a very long training program.* A short training program may mean there is a shallow foundation for the system. A long program means that the concept may be too difficult to teach.

10. *Any franchisor you don't feel good about.* The rule of thumb is to know your franchisor. Franchising is like a marriage. You wouldn't marry someone you just met in an afternoon.

A word about gut feelings. You may have carefully gathered your research on your chosen franchise and found that the numbers add up, the company has satisfied franchisees, the financials look good, the market research appears to be strong, but you still have a nagging hesitancy to move forward with the deal. For some reason, your gut isn't satisfied.

Maybe you don't personally like the franchisor or you aren't sure that the location the franchisor has in mind for you is the best one. It doesn't matter what the reason is, but it does matter that you stop and listen to your inner voice. This is not the time to ignore your gut feelings and plunge ahead. You have too much riding on this decision.

Instead, back away, give it some more time, and look elsewhere. You may end up coming back and signing on, but only when it feels right and after all the information is in.

4

Preparing the loan proposal

Let's face it: If you don't have the money, you don't open your doors. And the amount of money is significant, although the total project costs to acquire and develop a franchise will vary widely from franchisor to franchisor and from industry to industry. For example, a fast-food chain could cost well over $500,000 for construction, equipment, and inventory, whereas a temporary services placement franchise might be opened for under $50,000.

The typical franchisee borrows at least some of the money to start a franchise. You usually don't borrow all of it for a number of reasons. For one thing, you shouldn't leave yourself totally exposed to the ups and downs of the market. You need some resources in reserve to help you through the inevitable rough times that will come your way no matter how successful you may be. You will also have to have some assets in reserve in case you need another cash infusion down the road.

This last point is not generally well understood, even by very successful businesspeople. A business requires cash to grow. For example, you need to hire people, or to buy a new piece of equipment or the real estate for a new location. With luck, you will find a franchise you like and look forward to opening another outlet, or even two or three. This happens often. Unless you are extraordinarily successful, you will not be able to generate enough cash on hand for these expansion efforts.

And you cannot make a change out of nothing. Even if you hire someone and put him or her to work right away, you will certainly have expenses—health insurance, early salaries, and so on—that you will have to pay before that person starts to generate extra income for you. The same is true for a piece of equipment. You'll have to lay out the money for it (in some form or other) before it starts generating new revenues for you.

It may well be that you are so successful in your new venture that you will have enough new assets to borrow against. That is still a very optimistic situation and not something you should assume. You won't want to overextend yourself by borrowing against future business, even if you find a lender willing to go that far with you. So keep a little in reserve for rainy days and bright days when you can go back to your lending officer to say, "Well, things are going so well, I want to borrow for my new store."

The amount of capital required will dictate the type of loan that must be obtained as well as the information to be contained in the loan proposal. Regardless of which type of franchise you plan to open, the primary loan proposal that must be prepared should follow this basic outline:

Summary of the Request. This is an overview of the history of the franchisor and the would-be franchisee making the proposal, a summary of the key terms of the franchise agreement, the amount of capital needed, proposed repayment terms, the intended use of the capital, and the collateral available to secure the loan.

The summary of request is a kind of table of contents and short version of what is to follow. You will want to write a draft of it as you start out and then go back over it to bring it into line with what you have already done. Properly used, the summary is a good guide for you as you work out the kind of financing you want to do.

It is like the summary of a business plan and is itself a kind of business plan in miniature. In the course of writing your proposal, you will be testing your acumen, your skills, your confidence. You'll want to be sure that you can deliver on every part of your plan.

History of the Borrower. The history covers more than just your own business history. It will include a brief background of the business offered by the franchisor because that is a major part of your new business. Here is where the franchise concept can help you enormously because at least one of the partners in your enterprise is (or should be) a proven success. The franchisor's history of success with its other franchisees will help to convince the borrower that your business proposal is sound and well tested. This is a good part of the battle.

The history will need to project into the future to show how the franchise will be developed in the local market by the franchisee. You want to show that it has a sound expectation of success, with some useful facts and figures to back you up. Have you gone out on the street at your proposed location to see what the traffic is like? Have you surveyed other businesses that might use your service and gotten some letters of support, or even commitment, from them? All of this information is germane to your success and should be included in your loan proposal.

This section will also give the business background of the principal(s) of the proposed franchise (education, experience, business acumen). It will cover the franchisor's stage of development and plans for growth in the franchisee's marketplace, a list of proposed key customers, suppliers and service providers, management structure and philosophy, plant and facility, and an overview of the key products, support, and services offered by the franchisor.

Market Data. Market data include not only the informal surveys you might have undertaken, but a good deal of information that the franchisor should already have at hand. You need to pass this information on to the lender. It should include, so far as they are available:

- *An overview of trends in the industry.* The lender will want to know whether you are catching the beginning of an important marketing trend or trailing behind a well-developed competitor. If you are in a fairly crowded market—fast food, for example—are you working with a product that has a lot of potential and that has proven appeal? Who would have thought 15 years ago that pizza would overtake hamburgers as America's favorite snack food? Tom Monaghan of Domino's thought so, and those franchisees who started with him then are multimillionaires now.

- *The size of the market and its potential.* That would include the franchisor's market share nationally, including how much of the country is already penetrated. If the franchisor is relatively young, there need to be projections based on actual experience in other franchise locations.

- *Assessment of the competition.* If you are second in the market, the competition could put you out of business. The franchisor (and you) surely have thought of ways to avoid that, to take a disadvantage and make it into an advantage. Part of the strength you can offer is what proprietary advantages the franchisor has in the way of trademarks, well-developed and patented product or process, and so on. You also need to assess the impact of nonfranchised competition.

- *Local public relations and advertising strategies.* How are you going to get known and how much is that going to cost? Do you have clever promotional ideas? Some franchisees are better at advertising and promotion than franchisors and have taken the lead in providing clever ideas for the franchisor. Here you will just hit the high points because you'll go into more detail in the marketing and promotional strategy section.

- *An overview of trends in the industry, the size of the market, the franchisor's market share, an assessment of the local franchised and nonfranchised competition (direct and indirect), proprietary advantages of the franchisor, local public relations and advertising strategies, market research studies, and future industry prospects.*

Site Analysis.   This section should describe the key features of the actual or proposed site of the business, including a summary of the key lease terms as well as any supporting demographic information, traffic pattern studies, construction timetable, zoning issues, parking arrangements, and any other data that would be helpful to the lender. If the site is to be located in a mall or shopping center, then this section should include a discussion of any common area charges, merchant's associations, and an overview of any directly or indirectly competitive (or synergistic) tenants. If you are acquiring an existing franchised business, then any past performance data as well as copies of the acquisition documents can be included in this section.

Marketing and Promotional Strategy.   This section should describe the overall marketing strategy to be implemented by the franchisee. It should discuss the type and frequency of the advertising that will be used, the types of promotions and public relations to be used, and the level of support provided by the franchisor. For example, if the franchisor has established national, regional, or local advertising cooperatives, then the terms of membership should be discussed. Any mandatory local advertising required by the franchise agreement should also be included in this section. Finally, any special events, such as grand openings, special sales, or promotions should be included here.

Financial Information. Financial statements of the franchisor, personal financial statements of the franchisee, credit references, and the last 2 years' tax returns should be included in this section. The role of the capital requested with respect to the franchisee's plans for initial opening and growth, an allocation of the loan proceeds, and the franchisee's ability to repay must be carefully explained. The lender is going to want to see that the franchisee is bringing a certain amount of equity in the form of cash to the table, typically at least 25 percent. Most lenders will prefer to provide financing for the "hard assets," such as equipment and inventory, and will want the franchisee to be in a position to pay for the initial franchisee fee, training costs, and initial marketing costs. The discussion of the franchisee's ability to service the debt must be supported by a 3-year projected cash flow statement, typically presented on a monthly basis and well-supported assumptions and footnotes. In certain cases, the lender will want to know whether the franchisor is willing to execute a third-party guaranty or a remarketing agreement for the franchisee's equipment, signs, and inventory.

Schedule and Exhibits. A schedule of supporting documents must be made available to the lender for inspection upon request, such as lease agreements, franchise offering documents, and franchise agreements, shareholder agreements, and partnership agreements. The lender may also ask for copies of insurance policies, business licenses, and a variety of other documents that may be pertinent. Résumés of the franchisee, recent articles about the franchisor, the franchisor's marketing literature, and pictures of the franchisor's products or typical site should be appended.

Before submitting the loan proposal to the bank of your choice, you need to understand what the lender is looking for. Banks are in the business of selling money. Capital is the principal product in their inventory. Bankers, however, don't like risk. The shareholders and board of directors of any bank expect that loan officers will take all necessary steps to minimize the risk to the institution in each transaction and obtain the maximum protection in the event of default.

There are also stricter federal rules about lending money since the savings and loan and banking debacles of the late 1980s. Bankers expect much more scrutiny of loans. Therefore, the types of loans available to prospective franchisees, the terms and conditions of loan agreements, and the steps taken by the bank to protect its interest all have a direct relationship to the level of risk that is perceived by the lending officer and the loan committee. The types of loans and tips for negotiating lending transactions are covered in Chap. 13, so we'll spend our time here looking at related issues in preparing a loan proposal.

Preparing for debt financing

The cost of your loan—and whether it is approved at all—depends on how convincingly you demonstrate that the risk is minimal. For a prospective franchisee, this will mean a loan proposal package that demonstrates that the franchisor is established and experienced, with a good track record and a strong franchise management team.

You'll need financial statements of the franchisor and personal statements of the franchisee, and projections that demonstrate the ability to service the debt. To show that you know how to operate, you'll need to show that the franchisor has well-developed relationships with local suppliers, distributors, and employees and an understanding of the trends in the franchisee's local marketplace.

Many commercial loan officers will apply the traditional test of the four "Cs" of creditworthiness: character (reputation and honesty), capacity (business acumen and experience), capital (ability to meet debt-service payments), and collateral (access to assets that can be liquidated in the event of a default).

Lenders will want to know that you are willing to put your own assets at risk before they put the bank's assets at risk. Your willingness to pledge your home or other key asset as collateral for the loan demonstrates a genuine commitment to the lender. The willingness to pledge assets, together with a franchisor with a strong track record and your own personal résumé demonstrating management experience, will go a long way in getting your loan approved.

The commercial lender will always want the following questions answered in meetings as well as in the loan proposal package:

Who is the borrower?

How much capital is needed and when?

How will the capital be allocated? For what specific purposes?

How will the borrower service its debt obligations (e.g.,

application and processing fees, interest, principal or balloon payments)?

What protection (e.g., tangible and intangible assets to serve as collateral) can the borrower provide the bank in the event that the franchisee is unable to meet its obligations?

The answers to these questions are all designed to assist the bank in an assessment of the general risk factors in the proposed financing to the franchisee. However, these answers are also designed to provide the commercial loan officer with the information necessary to persuade the loan committee to approve the transaction.

Your loan officer, once convinced of your creditworthiness, will then serve as an advocate on behalf of the business in presenting the loan proposal to the bank's loan committee. The loan documentation, terms, rates, and covenants (discussed in more detail in Chap. 13), which the loan committee will specify as a condition to making the loan, will be directly related to the ways in which the applicant is able to demonstrate its ability to mitigate and manage risk as described in its formal loan proposal.

Tips for presenting data about the franchisor

One of the most critical sections of the loan proposal is the presentation of the strengths and weaknesses of the franchisor by the prospective franchisee/borrower. This is primarily because the affiliation of the prospective franchisee with the training and ongoing support offered by the franchisor will generally dramatically decrease the chance of the franchisee's going out of business, thereby reducing the risk to the lender.

The lender will be looking for a series of characteristics in determining the strength of the franchisor, such as:

- Trends within the franchisor's industry affecting the long-term viability of the franchisor's products or services.
- The financial and operational track record of other franchisees and company-owned units of the franchisor (e.g., revenue levels, breakeven analysis, profitability, etc.).
- The willingness of the franchisor to offer "comfort" to the lender in the form of guaranties, subleases, or remarketing agreements.

- The depth and experience of the franchisor's management team.
- The quality of the training and support offered by the franchisor.
- The franchisor's plans for expansion and growth (an overly aggressive plan may scare off a lender, and an overly slow plan may raise concerns about the viability of the franchising program).
- The "word on the street" about the reputation of the franchisor in its industry, among its franchisees, and among other lenders and landlords.
- The litigation and arbitration history of the franchisor, especially in disputes with its franchisees.
- The strength of the franchisor's intellectual property (e.g., trademarks, patents, and trade secrets).

5

Tips from franchise lenders

The common opinion among would-be franchisees is that bankers hate them. This isn't true, of course, although the lenders we talked with admitted that they hate the way entrepreneurs approach them for money.

It helps to keep in mind that bankers are fairly conservative when it comes to lending other people's money, whereas entrepreneurs are risk takers at heart, and they have trouble understanding why everyone around them doesn't agree with their approach.

Even though the banking industry is still skittish about making loans to businesses—small or large—the bank lenders we spoke with claim that tendency is changing in spite of the fact that the harsh lessons learned from the 1980s continue to influence lending decisions.

The bankers' wariness has its roots in the freewheeling lending climate of the 1980s when banks and lending institutions issued a host of ill-conceived loans to real estate entities, corporate raiders, oil drillers, and developing countries. Many of those loans—especially the ones made for real estate projects—went sour when the real estate market bottomed out. Borrowers defaulted and the banks were left with properties they couldn't sell.

The federal government was forced to allocate nearly $100 billion to bail out the savings and loans and set aside a $70 billion line of credit for cleaning up the banks. Tough new banking regulations were put into place to prevent future bad situations.

Between complying with the stricter regulations and being overly careful in qualifying new loan applicants, small business owners and would-be entrepreneurs find themselves caught in the middle. Even though the lending market is tough for small and new businesses, there are ways to approach your banker that will give you the best possible chance of getting money when you need it.

The real challenge for loan applicants is to find ways to bridge the relationship between them and the banker. If the banker's motto in the 1990s is "know your customer," then the motto for all businesses in this decade should be "know your banker."

Getting to know you

If there is one thing you take away from this chapter, we hope it is "know your banker." Gone are the days when you could simply apply for a loan and an unknown loan officer processed the application in your favor. The 1990s is a decade in which all the old rules of doing business apply—get to know your customer, and in this case, get to know your banker and allow him or her to get to know you.

So how do you get to know your banker? Start by making an appointment to see him or her. Introduce yourself, share your business goals, and begin the process of educating the individual about the concept of franchising.

Most bankers know very little about franchising, even though there is a movement towards allowing one person on a bank's staff to "specialize" in requests for franchising financing. Your job is to teach your banker about the concept of franchising, as well as about the franchise you want to own.

Lenders agree that there is no such thing as too much information about yourself, your background, and the business you want to own. Says Don Ervin, a financial consultant, bankers look for what they call qualified loan applicants, which is another way of saying that the banker knows a lot about the borrower and the business.

As you develop an ongoing relationship with your banker, be sure to share your past work experiences even if they don't directly apply to the franchise you want to buy. Bankers like to see some experience, regardless of the relevancy to your future business.

During this talking stage, be as open as you can about your personal financial situation, your family situation, what assets you plan to bring to the deal, and how you think your franchise will add to the community.

If it makes sense (or if it is possible), invite your banker for an on-site visit to your franchise location. Remember, the more the banker knows about you and your business, the stronger a case he or she can make when your application comes before the loan committee.

No surprises, please

Lenders don't like surprises. That's why they advise all loan applicants to keep them informed of what is happening in their financial lives—both the good and the bad.

If you have run into a snag in your attempts to buy a franchise, let your banker know that. Explain your situation—whatever it is—so that your banker will know what you are up against. Don't wait until you are desperate for money before you go to your bank for a loan. Bankers want to be part of your growth, slow and steady, but they don't appreciate last minute rushes.

Keep your banker aware of what is happening in your business and in the franchise community. If you see an article that is particularly informative, clip it out and send it along. That way your banker will learn about your business from *you,* not through the office grapevine, or worse, at the loan committee presentation.

The last thing you want is to have a member of the bank's loan committee raise a question about your business that your loan officer can't answer because you haven't kept him or her informed.

Bankers also want to know how you are going to make the business work, so be open about this area. Be specific about how much of your own money you plan to invest and how you plan to use the proceeds of the loan. Any marketing plans or long-term growth projections are likewise useful.

Lenders also advise that you provide a detailed personal financial statement, which includes a listing of your assets and liabilities. This gives the banker an idea about your ability to repay the loan.

Finally, anticipate questions before they are asked. If you don't have the answer, promise to get it and be sure to follow through. Bankers are not magicians and they resent being asked to go to bat for you when you haven't held up your end of the informational bargain.

Communicate!

This may appear to be too simplistic a point to make, but lenders repeatedly mention communication as the one area of needed improvement among loan applicants. Simply put: They want you to talk to them.

What does that mean? Telephoning them weekly just to chat about where you are in the franchise purchase process, or updating them about a new development in the franchise product or service, or simply asking them if they have any questions about your business, your background, or your application.

Bankers admit that they don't like being contacted *only* when the client has a financial problem. They want to hear about the ongoing good news in your business life, as well as the bad. If your banker has a true sense of what is going on with you and your business, he or she is better able to help you out of the occasional rough spots.

Accept the fact that bankers don't know everything about your business, so the more you can tell them the better off you will be. Educate your banker.

Shopping around

Should you shop around for a bank? You may have to. Not all banks have an understanding of franchising, and even fewer have a person on staff who is devoted to franchise lending. Canadian banks and lending institutions in Great Britain are far ahead of their American counterparts in this area. There are substantial departments devoted to franchise lending in both countries banking systems.

Part of the problem in this country has to do with the fact that there isn't one centralized banking system, as there is in Canada. Therefore, each bank functions independently. This can work in your favor, however.

Start first with your local banks. Because your franchise will be a *local* business, your chances of appealing to the bank's sense of community support is heightened.

Second, check to see if there is anyone in the bank who has dealt with franchise financing in the past. If so, this person, no matter who he or she is, should be your first stop.

You may find that you receive a cool reception at several banks. No matter. Keep trying. If you find that banks simply are not going to offer you help, then consider other lending institutions such as The Money Store, Franchise Funding Corporation, and the others listed in the appendixes in the back of this book. If you can locate a bank that is an SBA-approved lender, that will improve your chances for funding.

After you have located a bank, be sure to find out what documentation is needed for the application. Some banks require a 3- to 5-year past financial history along with a 3-year projection of the business sales; others do not. Wrong documentation for a loan creates delays in processing. (See Fig. 5-1.)

The seven "Cs"

In the past, bankers looked at what was known as the four "Cs" of your creditworthiness—character, capacity, capital, and collateral. In other words, how much money did you have to bring to the transaction, how would you pay back the loan, and what assets were you able to offer the bank as security against your loan?

These are still considered important elements of the loan application, but today lenders are extending the criteria used when evaluating a loan application. There are a host of considerations that come into play now, and some lenders say that there are seven elements that combine to cement the relationships between the banker, the business, and the community. Here they are.

1. *Capital.* What kind of capital is in your business? Where did it come from? What kind of work has it done so far in the funding of the business?

2. *Capacity.* Bankers will want to know about the leadership and experience of the people in your business. What kind of payments have they made on past credit? How much depth is in the business structure in leadership and experience?

3. *Character.* Most bankers have drifted away from examining the character of the business and its owners during the past years because of the bankers' preoccupation with collateral, says Ervin, but now bankers want to know about what they call the true entrepreneurial ego of an applicant, or whether a businessperson is proactive or reactive. Be prepared to share your personal working traits with the banker. What are the values and the principles of the people in your business? If you have a mission statement, be sure to include it. Ervin advises not to say anything to the banker that you can't back up either in research or historical data on your company.

4. *Commitment.* Bankers want to see a demonstration of loyalty and dedication to the business from you and your employees. This commitment may be in the form of the amount

SMALL BUSINESS LOAN APPLICATION

THIS APPLICATION WHEN COMPLETED
DOES NOT OBLIGATE EITHER PARTY IN ANY MANNER

PERSONAL DATA

Applicant Name _____
          First   Middle   Last

Social Security # _____   Date of Birth _____

Marital Status   M   S

Home Address _____

City _____   State_____   Zip_____

Home Phone (__) _____   Business Phone (__) _____

Is Co-Applicant your spouse?   [ ]   Yes   [ ] No

Co-Applicant's Name _____
               First   Middle   Last

Social Security # _____   Date of Birth _____

Marital Status: M   S

Home Address _____

City _____   State_____   Zip_____

Home Phone (__) _____   Business Phone (__) _____

APPLICANT'S EDUCATION HISTORY

Dates of Attendance	School/College	Major	Degree

Fig. 5-1   A sample loan application.

CO-APPLICANT'S EDUCATION HISTORY

Dates of
Attendance   School/College   Major   Degree

_____
_____
_____

APPLICANT'S EMPLOYMENT HISTORY

Dates   Annual
From-To   Company   Position   Income

_____
_____
_____

CO-APPLICANT'S EMPLOYMENT HISTORY

Dates   Annual
From-To   Company   Position   Income

_____
_____
_____

Other business affiliations (officer, director, owner, partner, etc.)

_____
_____

Have you ever failed in business or filed voluntary or involuntary bankruptcy? [ ] Yes [ ] No
(If yes, please list when, where, circumstances, including any remaining liabilities.)

_____

Are there any lawsuits pending against you? [ ] Yes [ ] No

If yes, please describe: _____
_____
_____

Fig. 5-1   (Continued) A sample loan application.

Have you ever been charged with or convicted of a crime or act of moral turpitude?
[ ] Yes   [ ] No

If yes, please describe: _____
_____
_____

Are you a U.S. Citizen? [ ] Yes [ ] No

If no, in which country do you hold a citizenship: _____

Where will the funds come from to meet the requirements of the repayment of the loan?
Enter source and dollar amounts: _____

Do you plan to have a partner (other than your spouse or co-applicant)? [ ] Yes   [ ] No

PERSONAL RESIDENCE

Type of Property: _____

Date Purchased/Price:_____

Estimated Current Value:_____

Mortgage Lender:_____   Amount:_____

Monthly Payment: _____

DEPOSIT ACCOUNT INFORMATION

Personal bank accounts and savings and loan deposits carried at:

Bank _____   Contact Name _____

Account No. _____   Phone No. (__)_____

Bank _____   Contact Name _____

Account No. _____   Phone No. (__)_____

Fig. 5-1   (Continued) A sample loan application.

Bank _____   Contact Name _____

Account No. _____   Phone No. (__)_____

ASSETS

Cash in Banks _____

Savings and Loan Deposits _____

Investments: Bonds and Stocks _____

Accounts and Notes Receivable _____

Real Estate Owned (other than residence) _____

Automobiles: Year _____ Make _____

Personal Property and Furniture _____

Life Insurance Cash Surrender Value _____

Other Assets - itemize _____

Profit Sharing _____

Retirement Funds _____

Attach Current Personal Financial Statement

TOTAL ASSETS _____

LIABILITIES

Notes Payable: Name Payee

to banks _____

to relatives _____

to others _____

Fig. 5-1   (Continued) A sample loan application.

Installment Accounts Payable:

Automobile _____

Other-(Attach Separately) _____

Other accounts payable _____

Mortgage payable on Real Estate _____

Unpaid Real Estate Taxes _____

Unpaid Income Taxes _____

Secured Loans _____

Loans on Life Insurance Policies _____

Credit Cards:_____ Avg. Monthly:_____

Other debts - itemize _____

TOTAL LIABILITIES _____
NET WORTH (Assets - Liabilities) _____

TOTAL LIABILITIES
& NET WORTH _____

SCHEDULE OF NOTES AND ACCOUNTS PAYABLE

Includes installment debts, revolving charge accounts, bank notes, etc. Specify any assets pledged as collateral indicating the liabilities which they secure:

To Whom Payable	Date	Amount Due	Monthly Interest Payment	Assets Pledged As Security

Fig. 5-1   *(Continued) A sample loan application.*

BUSINESS PLAN AND OPERATION

Nature of Business to be Operated: _____
_____
_____

Total Projected Costs to Open the Business: _____

Projected Monthly Operating Revenues and Expenses:

      Sources of Revenue: _____
                                _____
                                _____

      Operating Expenses: _____
                                  _____
                                  _____

      Projected Pre-Tax
      Monthly Profit: _____
                                  _____
                                  _____

PLEASE ATTACH TO THIS APPLICATION A COPY OF YOUR BUSINESS PLAN, PRO FORMA FINANCIAL STATEMENTS AND ANY OTHER EXHIBITS OR ATTACHMENTS (E.G. COPIES OF FRANCHISE AGREEMENTS, LEASES, ETC.) WHICH WOULD BE RELEVANT TO THE EVALUATION BY OUR LOAN COMMITTEE.

I certify that the information I have provided on this application, together with any attachments or exhibits thereto, is complete and correct. I hereby authorize the Lender or its authorized agent to obtain verification of any of the above information and I authorize the release of such information to the Lender or its authorized agent.

Signature of Applicant_____   Date_____

Signature of Applicant_____   Date_____

Fig. 5-1   (Continued) A sample loan application.

of capital you have invested thus far, or it may be the amount of time you and your employees have devoted to the business.

5. *Customers.* When things are going well, the economy is extremely strong, and there is plenty of collateral, bankers don't ask questions like "Does the community need your product or service?" Times have changed that. Now you should plan on answering questions about the competition in your market: Why does your business stand out, what is your image, and how do you intend to maintain your market share?

6. *Community.* Bankers will want to know how this business relates to the community in areas such as the environment and job creation. Local banks are part of the business community in which they operate—they are community-oriented businesses themselves. As such, they have a responsibility to help local businesses because if the community doesn't survive, the banks don't survive.

7. *Collateral.* Because bankers have been disappointed with the major source of collateral to date—real estate—Ervin suggests that businesspeople avoid talking about collateral during the loan application meeting for as long as possible. Instead, lenders advise, put your best foot forward in the banking relationship by focusing on the other "Cs" as evidence of your ability to make your business successful, enabling you to pay back what you are asking for. Then offer your collateral as secondary protection for the bank.

For more information on how to please a banker, read *Steps to Small Business Financing,* published jointly by the American Bankers Association and the National Federation of Independent Business. The booklet reviews what you need to know before applying for a loan. Single copies are available for $2.50 by sending a check to Small Business Financing, NFIB Foundation, Box 7575, San Mateo, CA 94403.

6
Sources
of financing

After you've looked at the amount you need to purchase a franchise and the resources you currently have, you're almost certainly left with a gap to fill. And filling that gap is what financing is all about.

Debt versus equity

There are two kinds of financing: debt or equity (see Fig. 6-1). With debt financing you borrow money. Borrowing means you're using someone else's money and paying rent on it. It has some advantages. If you're incorporated, you can deduct the interest at the corporate level. For investors, the properly secured loan is a safe investment.

There are all kinds of "instruments" of debt, from straightforward loans, second mortgages, and leases to private stock placements, debentures secured by the company's general credit, and bonds secured by assets. These latter are for good-sized corporations with a track record, not start-ups. But who knows? One of these fine days you might want to consider such instruments.

Equity sources	Debt sources
Savings	Bank loans
Family and friends	Family and friends
Investors	Credit cards
Venture capitalist	SBA guarantee
Partners	Insurance loan
SBIC	Line of credit

Fig. 6-1 Sources of financing.

The advantage of debt financing is that you keep all the ownership of your company in your own hands. The disadvantage is that you may stretch yourself thin, or, in the worst case, lose all your security if the business fails.

Equity financing means you sell a share of your ownership—and that means a reduction in control. This isn't so bad in the case of a franchise because you are already following a format, and there are not that many ways an outside person might tell you what to do. On the other hand, you may lose your majority interest, and then it will be possible for the equity partner to exclude you from any daily operations altogether.

The most common form of equity financing is the sale of stock. You may sell partnership interests, either formally or informally.

The same people can offer both debt and equity financing. First we'll look at some of the sources of money and suggest what kind of financing each might come up with.

It's in the bank

Your first impulse in starting your own franchise is to find the money at the bank. Sometimes that's the right idea, sometimes not.

The truth is, your bank loan is probably only going to be a part of your entire financing package. You will still need a substantial number of assets of your own to get the bank to come up with the money.

Collateral is as hard to find as the liquid assets, and especially in hard times. The good news is that everyone wants to see small businesses succeed (and that is what a franchisee is running) and that franchising itself lends a great deal of credibility for a first-time entrepreneur. The trouble is, too many people don't dig enough into all the methods of financing that are available. Even those that we suggest here won't be all the different ways you can do it. Resourceful businesspeople are always coming up with something new.

Your own resources

Your first source of money is yourself. Your first idea is to go to *savings*. You may not wish to use the money itself, but it is an asset against which you can borrow.

Other assets are possessions—a home, a car, a boat, furnishings, jewelry. Take an inventory of these. They aren't necessarily liquid assets, but they can be collateral for a loan.

You have already done a quick financial survey in Chap. 2. The assets you listed point to your borrowing power if you go to traditional sources. Your home is the first place you look. You may have considerable equity in it, and you need to make an honest appraisal of its market value in order to establish that. If you choose to take out a home equity loan as part of your financing, you need to have a formal appraisal, and you don't want nasty surprises.

You could sell your house outright and have the cash in hand. (Some franchises you might want to buy may not be available where you are living, and so you would have to sell your house anyway.) The problem with this approach is that you still have to live somewhere, and you will have to deal with the issue of capital gains. It may be that new laws will allow you to reinvest money from a home sale in a new business, but you can't count on changes in the law to help you out.

Other possessions are more difficult to turn into cash or collateral. Automobiles are notoriously quick to lose their value, but at least some of it can be counted in your net worth as loan collateral. Furnishings and jewelry, as well as boats and other luxury items, will need to be appraised by a reputable appraiser.

One other important factor in all this is you. Any lender or provider of capital is going to look at the skills, ability, and ethics of the person asking for the money. Have you had a good history of paying debts? Have you been timely in payments? If you had difficulty, did you keep the lender informed and make your best efforts to get back to timely payments? These are important issues, and your own track record is your essential proof.

One franchisee, Craig Yalch of Michigan, decided to open a franchise of BriteTech in his area. The company specializes in cleaning ceilings and other surfaces damaged by pollutants. When he and a partner decided to buy the franchise, they went to the bank with a unique approach. They demonstrated the service at the bank for the loan committee. After seeing the product and service in action, the bank financed the whole franchise. So originality and talent are important.

Once all this is together, you need to talk to a bank officer, preferably one you've dealt with for a while.

Many banks are beginning to specialize in small-business loans in the range of $75,000 to $800,000. They don't advertise (they don't have to), so you'll have to do a lot of asking at a lot of banks to find one.

Of course, it's a good idea to go to your own bank first, especially if you have a good working relationship already or if you and your business are well known and have a history with that bank. Of course, your bank may still not be interested in making the loan for many reasons, and you may well have to go looking for another institution.

Bank experts say that you should find a bank officer who is experienced at making commercial loans. "Deal with the highest level you can," says Joseph A. Campanella, director of the corporate-finance department of the Koptis Organization, a Cleveland business consulting firm.

When you find a bank that is interested, and an officer who will listen, don't get scared. You have a good plan and a franchise with its own track record of success. Present your case effectively.

Rather than an outright business loan, you may wish to arrange for a *line of credit,* either secured or unsecured. An unsecured line of credit is difficult to get for a new business, no matter how much confidence you have in it. Franchises are a little easier than other businesses, but much depends on the quality of your business plan. The secured line of credit, such as a home equity line, is easier to get because the bank has a reasonable assurance of getting its money back some way.

Sometimes a line of credit is the best way to go because you only pay interest on the money you use as you use it. This is particularly useful if you are doing renovations or building changes, which can take a lot of time. All that time translates into cost if you already have taken the money in a lump sum, and the money is doing no work for you. The line of credit avoids that.

Another source of credit, though an extremely expensive one, is a *credit card.* Using credit cards is not something we recommend except for unusual or unexpected expenses. But in your planning, you might do well to find some relatively inexpensive credit cards you can obtain before you quit your current job or actually get into the launch of the business.

You can also arrange a loan or line of credit against your *insurance policies.* These are available directly from the insurance company, and the interest rate is usually fairly low (it is, after all, your own money that you are borrowing). This should be a short-term kind of loan as well because you don't want your policies questionable when you (or your family) need them.

While we are on the category of loans, you might want to consider a couple of other sources. One is your *credit union,* which also is in the business of lending money. The interest rates will be favorable, and a credit union may be a little easier to borrow from than a bank. Of course you will have to demonstrate the track record they need to prove to their own lending committee that you are a good risk.

The U.S. Small Business Administration (SBA) offers *SBA loan guarantees,* which we cover in detail in Chap. 7. The SBA itself does not lend money; it guarantees loans as a last resort for businesspeople who have been turned down by conventional sources. There has been considerable heat generated about these loan guarantees, but they will probably be given for some time.

For information on SBA loan guarantees or other SBA programs, call their Answer Desk toll-free at (800) 368-5855 between 8:30 a.m. and 5 p.m. EST. In Washington, DC, call 653-7561. There is also more information on the SBA and the programs it administers in the following chapter.

Family and friends

One logical source of money is from your family or friends. These fine people believe in you (usually) and don't require the same kind of collateral that banks do. Banks are not family.

You should be very careful about such loans. It is best to present the business plan just as you would for a regular loan or for a pitch to any other investor. Even though your family or friends might give you money at the drop of a hat, what are you willing to give back to them? It isn't fair to use their money with no interest or return on their investment.

It also is important for your peace of mind that you do not take any money that would put your family or friends in a difficult financial position. Don't take their retirement savings or their college money. Even if you pay it back, you may find yourself delayed in doing so, and then they would be in a bind. Few family relationships and fewer friendships could stand such a strain.

In any case, make sure you give a note with terms of payment to those from whom you borrow. It's businesslike, it's a clear statement of intent that everyone can fall back on, and it's good discipline (it means you'll pay attention to the repayment terms).

Partners

You may be considering going into your franchise with a partner. Partners can be a good idea. You share the work and the risk—and the rewards.

If you are taking on a partner, you'll have a number of issues to deal with that have to do specifically with partnerships. On a personal level, you need to know that you can work well with this person, that your talents are complementary, and that you won't bug one another to death.

You should have a partnership agreement that spells out who does (and gets) what, what happens if one of you should want out or if both of you wants the franchise exclusively to yourself. You need to have a good lawyer work out this agreement.

Once you have assured yourself that you can work with someone else, then all that partner's resources are available. All your borrowing and investing power should double. If one partner has less money than the other, then some arrangement of the equity position should reflect that.

Investors

Investors are often very willing to consider franchises. Franchises have that excellent track record of success that we talked about in the first chapter, and they do have the kind of ongoing support which reduces the risks that an outright entrepreneur might face.

Investors are often called *venture capitalists,* but that is only one kind of investor. Friends and family are investors, they just aren't strangers. But not all investors are venture capitalists.

But we'll start with the "VCs" as they are called. The venture capital business is high risk. Even though the franchise route is less risky, VCs are going to charge you for the risk by taking a considerable portion of the equity. VCs will also expect to get their money back in a fairly short fixed time (usually 5 years).

For a list of venture capitalists, contact the National Venture Capital Association, 1655 North Fort Meyer Dr., NE, Suite 700, Arlington, VA 22209; (703) 528-4370.

Venture capital clubs are a little different from the venture capital company. They are attempts to formalize somewhat informal networks of "angels"—people who invest in entrepreneurial businesses that they hear about through friends or associates. For a list of venture capital clubs, write the Association of Venture Capital Clubs, Mary Woita, 1313 Farnam, Suite 132, Omaha, NE 68182; (402) 554-8381. There is also the Venture Capital Network, P.O. Box 882, Durham, NH 03824; (603) 743-3993.

You may also find investment loans through *financial companies,* but these can be risky. Unless you are hard pressed, leave these as a last resort. A reputable finance company should offer you a reasonable interest rate, although it will be quite a bit higher than a bank.

You might find some sources of investment in unusual places, like coworkers at your current job. They may also be wanting to start businesses of their own, or perhaps they might like to be partners in a small way in yours. You can structure the money as an investment (with appropriate equity given to them) or as a loan.

In the now-fashionable attempt to encourage the formation of small businesses, states and municipalities are suddenly pushing forward. They know that business is the ultimate source of the money for their services. More businesses in a town means more tax revenue, growth, and other good things. Not only are states and municipalities trying to provide the usual incentives for businesses to locate in their areas through tax breaks and help in complying with laws and regulations, they are also offering business loans. Many want to invest in start-ups through seed loans and venture capital—or equity financing.

The state of Maryland, for example, started an innovative program of equity financing for minority franchisees. The program was designed to make the state a partner with the starting franchisee, offer some expertise as well as money, and get enough profit to expand the program. So far, it's working.

Many states have started business incubators; Pennsylvania, South Carolina, and New Jersey, for example, are strong in this. Incubators are central locations—often in universities, but sometimes privately financed—that allow a number of start-ups to share costs. The incubators have centralized secretarial and printing, sometimes equipment, and usually an administrator who can offer all kinds of advice to help a company get started and stay on its feet. Your state department of commerce should be able to tell you about small-business loan and incubator programs.

Don't overlook your franchise partner

The franchisor will often provide some financial help to a qualified and capable potential franchisee. Potential franchisees in this rapidly growing system are not that easy to come by, and talent, energy, and enthusiasm are bankable qualities.

Remember, too, that the franchisor believes in its own product or service. The point of the franchise system is that the franchisee provides some time and money, which allows the system to grow more quickly than it would by using the franchisor's own money. But if it comes to making up a small percentage of the deficit out of its own capital, the franchisor often prefers to help a talented franchisee to losing that person to another franchisor.

Many franchisors will do some hand-holding through the process of searching for money. The Bike Line franchise has an in-house financial adviser who was a bank loan officer. The company, after the franchisee has come up with all the money he or she can, will give the bank first lien on the franchisee's inventory. If there is less than the franchise fee left to come up with, the company will take that back at a percentage or so above going rates for 3 years.

Sometimes a company will help with equipment costs or leasing. And on some occasions, if you are buying an existing franchise outlet, the company may set up a lease/purchase agreement, allowing you, in essence, to work for the company until you have proven yourself.

The good news is, if you are responsible and capable, there are many ways to find the money you need. Don't give up too easily.

7

Federal, state, and local financing programs

When you can't get a loan from your bank or other lending institution, it is time to consider alternative sources of financing—namely, federal, state and local programs designed to help the would-be entrepreneur get started.

These programs are not limited only to franchise buyers; the funds are available to all small business owners who need capital to purchase an asset, pay an expense, or make an investment. But franchisors and franchisees are discovering that these programs often meet their needs when conventional methods of borrowing are unavailable to them.

The language of lending for these nontraditional sources of money include the SBA 7(a) loan program, the SBA 504 direct loan program, the SBA small loan program, SBICs, SBLCs, BIDCOs; VetFran; micro loans; and CSBG, among others. Here are some definitions.

U.S. Small Business Administration

The U.S. Small Business Administration has several loan programs. *Section 7(a)* is the SBA's guaranteed loan program. Section 7(a) authorizes the SBA to offer guarantees on loans; 90 percent of the loan up to $155,000 and then 85 percent of the remainder up to a total loan amount of $750,000.

From a bank's standpoint, these are attractive types of loans; the bank's maximum exposure is only 15 percent and the loan is secured by the SBA.

The interest rate on these loans varies, depending on the term of the loan and how the funds are to be used. The terms range from 5 to 25 years, and the interest rate may not exceed the prime rate plus 2.75 percent.

You can use the funds for a number of things, including working capital; the purchase of buildings, equipment, inventory, supplies, and materials; expansion or renovation of existing facilities; construction of new facilities; and debt repayment.

When applying for an SBA-backed loan, be sure you are dealing with a bank that accepts them. A complete loan application would include:

- A solid business plan
- A thorough description of the business
- A financial statement (personal and business) that is dated within 90 days of the application
- A personal data sheet
- The loan amount and how you intend to use the money
- A projected profit and loss statement prepared by month for the next year
- Growth projections for the next 3 to 5 years

If you are applying for start-up financing, be prepared to have 30 to 50 percent of your own money to bring to the deal. One final criterion—you must have been turned down by at least one commercial lender.

For information on which banks in your areas are involved in the SBA guaranteed loan program, contact your regional SBA office. The addresses and telephone numbers of 10 regional offices follow:

Region 1
115 Federal St.
9th Floor
Boston, MA 02110
(617) 451-2023

Region 2
26 Federal Plaza
Room 31-08
New York, NY 10278
(212) 264-7772

Region 3
475 Allendale Rd.
Suite 201
King of Prussia, PA 19406
(215) 962-3700

Region 4
1375 Peachtree St., NE
5th Floor
Atlanta, GA 30367-8102
(404) 347-2797

Region 5
230 South Dearborn St.
Room 510
Chicago, IL 60604-1593
(312) 353-0359

Region 6
8625 King George Dr.
Building C
Dallas, TX 75235-3391
(214) 767-7643

Region 7
911 Walnut St.
13th Floor
Kansas City, MO 64106
(816) 426-3607

Region 8
999 18th St.
Suite 701
Denver, CO 80202
(303) 294-7001

Region 9
450 Golden Gate Ave.
San Francisco, CA 94102
(415) 556-7487

Region 10
2615 4th Ave.
Room 440
Seattle, WA 98121
(206) 442-8544

The *small loan program* is similar to the SBA 7(a) guaranteed loan program except there are incentives for lenders to make small loans—$50,000 or less—to businesses. Not all banks participate in this program, so first check with your banker or contact your local SBA office. As part of the incentive to make small loans to businesses, the SBA allows banks to charge higher interest rates—2 percent over prime for loans to

$25,000, and 1 percent over prime for loans from $25,000 to $50,000.

The *504 direct loan program* is designed for businesses that need a long-term loan in order to purchase fixed assets that will maintain or increase employment. It's a combination of a bank loan and a loan from the SBA through an authorized local development corporation (LDC) or through a regional or statewide certified development corporation (CDC).

This type of loan is for an established business that intends to expand, thus saving or increasing its employment numbers. Factors such as the borrower's debt-to-equity ratio are examined, and a formula is applied for determining the amount of the loan based on the salary levels of the employees saved or added within the next 2 years as a result of the loan.

If you are interested in financing through the 504 direct loan program, contact your local SBA office for information about the LDC or CDC nearest you.

Small business investment companies (SBICs) are privately run companies that are licensed by the SBA. They offer long-term debt or equity financing to small businesses; some SBICs specialize in minority lending. There are more than 500 SBICs. Your own bank may have an SBIC subsidiary, so it would be well for you to check.

Companies are eligible for SBIC financing if they have assets under $7.5 million, net worth under $2.5 million, and earnings of less than $250,000 during the last 2 years. The SBICs provide some expertise along with the capital. Because they are specifically set up to work with small businesses, they understand your goals and problems. Of course, if you don't have a good plan or demonstrate capable management, your reception will be no better than with any bank.

For a directory of SBICs and MESBICs (minority enterprise small business investment companies), write to the National Association of Small Business Investment Companies, 1156 15th St., NW, Suite 1101, Washington, DC 20005; (202) 833-8230. You can also get the *Directory of Operating Small Business Investment Companies* from the Associate Administrator–Finance & Investment, SBA, 1441 L St., NW, Washington, DC 20416. There is no charge for the SBA's directory.

Small business lending companies (SBLCs) are licensed by the SBA and operate under SBA's 7(a) loan program. Of the 16 such companies in the United States, eight are fairly active in offering loans to small businesses. Currently, there are four national SBLCs whose primary loan activities involve franchise start-ups and expansions.

Business and industrial development corporations (BIDCOs) provide long-term financing to small businesses, operate under state programs, and are backed by federal guarantees.

For more information about SBICs, SBLCs, and BIDCOs, write to or talk with your local SBA representative.

Help for veterans

If you are a veteran of America's armed forces and you want to buy a start-up franchise, a program exists that may help you accomplish that. Called the Veterans Transition Franchise Initiative (or VetFran), the program allows veterans to buy a franchise with no money down. The program is jointly cosponsored by Donald Dwyer, president of The Dwyer Group, a conglomerate of franchised businesses based in Waco, Texas; the U.S. Small Business Administration; and the International Franchise Association in Washington, DC.

Participating franchised companies agree either to reduce their up-front franchise fee for veterans or to finance up to 50 percent of the fee at market interest rates. Over 100 franchisors endorse the VetFran initiative.

The SBA speeds up loan-guarantee approvals for VetFran applicants so that they can pay the balance of the franchise fee (if any) plus any equipment costs.

All current veterans are eligible to apply for VetFran funding; the deadline is August 15, 1993. If you are on active duty now and become a veteran by August 15, 1993, you have 2 years from your discharge date to apply for the funding.

Franchise companies reserve the right to screen applicants to ensure that they meet the franchisor's ownership qualifications. To apply for VetFran, contact your local military processing center, a local SBA office, or The Dwyer Group at (817) 756-2122.

State and local funding programs

Many state and local governments have started financing initiatives to encourage small business development in their area. Unfortunately, each state and municipality refers to such programs differently; some are called micro loan programs, commercial lease programs, or community services block grant loans, among others.

In our research, we found that the state of Illinois developed the most comprehensive outreach program aimed at attracting qualified small business ownership to the state's cities and towns. By way of introducing smaller, lesser-known funding sources to you, we have listed the kinds of programs available in Illinois. It is our hope that by understanding the *content* of these programs you may discover similar opportunities in your own state.

It may be helpful to contact a small business resource center (SBRC) if your state has one. SBRCs are sponsored by the SBA and are often located at colleges or universities. Although SBRCs are not sources for direct funding of small businesses, the information available at the center may point you toward a funding program that works for you.

The following is an alphabetical listing by state of the addresses and telephone numbers of SBRCs.

University of Alabama
School of Business
901 15th St. South
Suite 143
Birmingham, AL 35294
(205) 934-7260

Anchorage Community College
430 West 7th Ave.
Suite 115
Anchorage, AK 99501
(907) 274-7232

Gateway Community College
108 North 40th St.
Phoenix, AZ 85034
(602) 392-5224

University of Arkansas
100 South Main St.
Suite 401
Little Rock, AR 72204
(501) 371-5381

Colorado Community College
600 Grant St. #505
Denver, CO 80203
(303) 894-2422

University of Connecticut
Room 422

368 Fairfield Rd.
Storrs, CT 06268
(203) 486-4135

University of Delaware
Suite 005
Purnell Hall
Newark, DE 19716
(302) 451-2747

District of Columbia
Howard University
2600 Sixth St., Room 128
Washington, D.C. 20059
(202) 806-1550

University of West Florida
1000 University Blvd.
Building 38
Pensacola, FL 32514
(904) 474-3016

University of Georgia
1180 East Broad St.
Athens, GA 30602
(404) 542-5760

Boise State University
College of Business
1910 University Dr.
Boise, ID 83725
(208) 385-1640

SBDC
620 East Adams St.
5th Floor
Springfield, IL 62701
(217) 785-6174

Iowa State University
Chamberlynn Bldg.
137 Lynn Ave.
Ames, IA 50010
(515) 292-6351

Wichita State University
1845 Fairmont
201 Clinton Hall
Wichita, KS 67208

(316) 689-3193

University of Kentucky
18 Porter Bldg.
Lexington, KY 40506
(606) 257-1751

Northeast Louisiana University
College of Business
Administration Bldg. 2-57
University Dr.
Monroe, LA 71209
(318) 342-2464

University of Southern Maine
246 Deering Ave.
Portland, ME 04102
(207) 780-4423

SBDC
217 East Redwood St.
10th Floor
Baltimore, MD 21202
(301)333-6608

University of Massachusetts
205 School of Management
Amherst, MA 01003
(413) 549-4930

Wayne State University
2727 Second Ave.
Detroit, MI 48201
(313) 577-4848

College of St. Thomas
Enterprise Center
1107 Hazeltine Blvd. #245
Chaska, MN 55318
(612) 448-8810

University of Mississippi
3825 Ridgewood Rd.
Jackson, MS 39211
(601) 982-6760

St. Louis University
3674 Lindell Blvd.
St. Louis, MO 63108
(314) 534-7204

University of Nebraska at Omaha
College of Business Administration Bldg.
60th & Dodge
Room 407
Omaha, NB 68182
(412) 554-2521

University of Nevada Reno
College of Business Administration
Room 411
Reno, NV 89557-0100
(702) 784-1717

University of New Hampshire
University Center
400 Commercial St.
Room 311
Manchester, NH 03101
(603) 625-4522

Rutgers University
180 University St.
3rd Floor
Newark, NJ 07102
(201)648-5950

Santa Fe Community College
PO Box 4187
Santa Fe, NM 87502-4187
(505) 471-8200

State University of New York (SUNY)
SUNY Central Administration S-523
Albany, NY 12246
(518) 473-5398

University of North Carolina
820 Clay St.
Raleigh, NC 27605
(919) 733-4643

University of North Dakota
217 South 4th St.
PO Box 1576
Grand Forks, ND 58206
(701) 780-3403

Columbus Chamber of Commerce
37 North High St.

Columbus, OH 43216
(614) 221-1321

Southeastern Oklahoma State University
Station A
Box 4194
Durant, OK 74701
(405) 924-0277

Lane Community College
Downtown Center
1059 Willamette St.
Eugene, OR 97401
(503) 726-2250

University of Pennsylvania
The Wharton School
3620 Locus Walk
Philadelphia, PA 19104

University of Puerto Rico
Mayaguez Campus
Box 5253
Mayaguez, PR 00709
(809) 834-3590

Bryant College
450 Douglas Pike
Smithfield, RI 02830
(401) 232-6111

University of South Carolina
College of Business Administration
Columbia, SC 29208
(803) 777-4907

University of South Dakota
Business Research Bureau
414 East Clarke St.
Vermillion, SD 57069
(605) 677-5272

Memphis State University
Fogelman Executive Center
Central & DeLoach
Suite 220W
Memphis, TN 38152
(901) 454-2500

University of Houston

401 Louisiana St.
Houston, TX 77002
(713) 223-1141

Community College
302 North Market #300
Dallas, TX 75202
(214) 747-0555

University of Utah
660 South 200 East
Room 418
Salt Lake City, UT 84111
(801) 581-7905

University of Vermont
Extension Service
Morrill Hall
Burlington, VT 05405
(802) 656-4479

Washington State University
441 Todd Hall
Pullman, WA 99164-4740
(509) 335-1576

SBDC
1115 Virginia St.
East Charleston, WV 25301
(304) 348-2960

University of Wisconsin
602 State St.
2nd Floor
Madison, WI 53703

Casper Community College
130 North Ash
Suite 2A
Casper, WY 82601
(307) 235-4825

To find out if programs like the ones offered in Illinois are available in your state, contact the state economic development department in your state and describe the kind of program you are interested in. It may be called something other than what is listed as follows, but the purpose and parameters of the program may be the same.

The *micro loan program* offers direct financing (in cooperation with private sector lenders) to small businesses at a below-market interest rate. The program is designed to create or retain jobs and to assist in expansion.

Up to 25 percent of the total cost may be borrowed, and a minimum of one job must be created for each $10,000 borrowed. Funds may be used for construction, for the purchase of land or buildings, inventory, equipment; and as working capital. A maximum amount of $100,000 may be borrowed, with 55 to 80 percent of the loan provided by the bank, 10 to 25 percent from the state's micro loan program, and 10 to 20 percent coming from owner equity.

The *commercial lease program* provides 100 percent financing for operating leases for equipment purchases of $25,000 to $200,000. Leases are for 5 years or less, depending on the useful life of the equipment. The lessee has the option to purchase the equipment at the end of the lease period, paying 10 percent of the purchase price.

This program requires that you have approximately 50 percent of the total amount requested in collateral. The interest rate equals prime plus 1.5 percent.

The *Community Services Block Grant Loan* uses Community Services Block Grant (CSBG) monies to make affordable, long-term, fixed-rate financing available to small businesses that start or expand in Illinois and that create employment opportunities for low-income workers. CSBG links public and private financing, which creates a blended interest rate for the borrower. The maximum loan amount is $500,000, and the money may be used to find fixed assets and working capital.

Disability business loans offer direct financing to small businesses at below-market interest rates in cooperation with private sector lenders. Their aim is to help disabled business owners create or retain jobs. Principal and interest payments for these loans are used to maintain a state revolving loan fund for use by other disabled-owned businesses. The loans cover 50 percent of the project cost up to $50,000. One job must be created or retained for every $15,000 of loan funds.

The *Illinois Development Finance Authority* (IDFA) finances equipment, land, and buildings, but not working capital. There are two funding methods available. The IDFA will fund 80 percent of the loan, with the remaining 20 percent coming from a bank or the business owner. The fixed interest rate is 7 percent, and the maximum loan amount is $25,000. Start-up businesses are eligible for this kind of funding.

The *revolving loan fund* requires 60 percent financing from the bank, 10 percent from the business owner, with the IDFA absorbing the remaining 30 percent.

The *modernization retooling* program offers longer-term, fixed-rate loans in cooperation with conventional lenders to finance machinery and equipment needed to modernize a business that is operating at a competitive disadvantage. Under this program, there are matching grants to businesses to help them hire consultants who can identify opportunities for improving productivity and profitability.

These are not the only state and local programs available throughout the country. There are other programs in your state or county that could be useful as you search for funding. Be tenacious when looking for these lesser known funding programs. They may not be easy to find, but if you don't give up, you may find what you need.

8

Financing for women and minorities

During the 1980s and early 1990s, women started twice as many small businesses as men. Although no statistics have been formally collected on the number of women who have chosen to enter business ownership through franchising, experts say the percentages are growing. Likewise, the franchise community is giving minority entrepreneurs more attention as potential franchise owners. Both women and minorities represent a large pool of talent that franchisors want to cash in on.

Right now, women franchisors account for just 11 percent of the total number of franchise companies—3100. Minority franchisees represent 8 percent of the overall franchisee pool, which is over 600,000 nationwide.

The primary reason that franchisors have not courted women and minority franchisee candidates with more enthusiasm is because both groups have traditionally not had access to the kind of funding necessary to own a franchise, says Susan Kezios, who owns and operates Women in Franchising, a Chicago-based firm that specializes in franchise ownership training for women and minorities.

Some franchise companies actively seek women and minority candidates and offer them help with the financing. More rivalry for qualified entrepreneurs is driving franchisors into the ranks of women and minorities who have the business and management background but not necessarily the financial wherewithal.

Among the most common financial barriers are lack of acceptable traditional collateral and lack of credit history. There are some negative perception barriers too. Women and minorities have been thought to lack commitment, experience, confidence, and effective women/minority business network support systems. This, of course, is far from being fact.

Studies conducted by Women in Franchising and minority and women business groups reveal that women and minority business owners are cautious risk takers who plan their growth with the use of small loans. They also don't traditionally use financial institutions for their growth capital.

So how do women and minorities get money? To some degree, in the same way other entrepreneurs locate funds—by blending financial resources. However, the difference for women and minorities is twofold: They often need training in *how* to approach a bank, and they need guidance on the kinds of special programs available just for them.

Blending your sources

Learning how to blend your sources of financing is the trick you must know if you are going to succeed in the financing game. Kezios says that it's not so important where you get your capital from, it's how you structure it.

That means starting with some money from you (your family, friends, savings), adding some funds available to you from a public sector program (such as those described in Chap. 7), and combining it with bank funding.

An advantage to blending your money with the bank's and public sector funds is that you can reduce your initial cash outlay and lower your monthly debt service. You'll get longer amortization with public sector loans, and you may have to pay interest for only part of that time, which will enhance the franchise's ability to survive.

Kezios says there are four places for women and minorities to find sources of capital: self-financing, the private sector, the public sector, and franchise companies.

Self-financing

Self-financing is what the term implies—drawing on capital that is liquid. This could include cash savings, money market funds, stocks, IRAs, other retirement funds, or loans from friends, family, or associates. The first step is to find out how much capital you have—whether it is $500 or $50,000. That's where the process starts.

Keep in mind that no franchisor is going to finance you 100 percent. They will want to see some financial commitment from you before they risk any of their resources. So put your pen to paper and list all the possible sources of capital that you have on hand that could be applied to your financing blend.

Private sector

Private sector financing is money that you borrow from banks or other lending institutions. How you approach a bank or lending institution may well determine the status of your loan.

Kezios maintains that women especially need help in how to interact with the banking community. She says you should start by describing the unique features of your business and figure out how to explain it in terms your lender can understand. Your job is to educate them on your specific service or product. You have a common language in the business plan and with your financial statements, which explain your allocation of resources.

When talking with your banker, don't say, "This is a new business." If it is a franchise, it is not a new business. It may be a new location in the market, but the business has been around for a while. Where your banker may need some help is in understanding the concept of franchising, as we discussed in Chap. 5. Take your time and be helpful.

Other points to consider include whether the bank has ever financed the type of business you're in. Besides the expertise of the staff, also check out the rest of the staff involved in making a loan decision. Sooner or later, bank employees make career changes, and the person you have been cultivating may have moved on. Kezios says it's smart to also get to know that person's supervisor.

How a loan decision is made

Banks and lending institutions make lending decisions in one of three ways: by loan committees, through tiered authority, or by individual authority.

Loan Committees.   In this format, your banker goes before a committee of bank managers to present the loan request and the managers vote on it.

Tiered Authority.   This gives individuals in the bank hierarchy personal discretion in granting loans up to a certain amount. Permission to lend larger amounts may require approval from someone the next step up the ladder. For example, your banker may have $50,000 of spending authority and be able to approve a loan for that amount. If you need $100,000, you may have to see your banker's supervisor. Someone on the next rung of the ladder can approve a higher amount, and so on.

Individual Authority.   This gives individual bankers the ability to approve the loan on their own. As in the tiered authority, there is a predetermined limit on how much a single banker can lend. The lender may be able to write you a check for $7500, but if you need $15,000, he or she has to get a second signature.

As banks consolidate and become more wary about those to whom they lend money, lending authority is more centralized, making individual authority less common than loan committees or tiered authority. Individual authority is rarely available to small borrowers, who are perceived as the worst credit risks.

So determine if the loan officer is going to be the person who will handle your account. If not, or if you determine that this person does not have enough authority to grant you the size loan you desire, say, "Thank you very much. You've been so helpful. Would you introduce me to your supervisor. That's what I came in to do today."

Support services

When you are looking for a bank, check out its supporting services. Is the bank conveniently located to your business? If you have a retail business that deposits $6000 of cash each day, the lender must be conveniently located. You're not going to travel across town to make daily cash deposits. Also, find out if the bank handles Visa, Mastercard, and American Express. If your franchise is a retail establishment, chances are you will need a bank that will give you merchant status.

You have some leverage

Ask to see the bank's Community Reinvestment Act (CRA) statement. A copy of the Community Reinvestment Act is contained in The Community Reinvestment Act of 1977, which requires financial institutions to demonstrate that their deposit facilities serve the convenience and needs of the communities in which they are chartered to do business.

The convenience and needs of the community includes the need for credit as well as deposit services. Regulated financial institutions have to assess the credit needs of the communities in their delineated market area and address those credit needs. All member banks have adopted a CRA statement for every community they serve.

The CRA statement may be a simple declaration of intent to lend to everyone in the bank's service area or a detailed description of the bank's involvement with small business lending, housing rehabilitation projects, and so on. A bank's CRA statement may also include a description of how its current efforts—including special credit-related programs—help to meet community credit needs.

Public sector

Public sector financing includes lending programs available through federal, state, county, and city agencies. Federal programs are typically administered through the U.S. Small Business Administration. When you go to a bank or a technical assistance program person to help you put your loan package together, the federal avenues are usually what they talk about.

But there are a number of lesser-known public sector financing programs available to women and minorities. See Chap. 7 for a description of many such programs. These loan programs offer significantly lower interest rates—sometimes as low as 3.5 percent—and the loan amount frequently is tied to the number of jobs your business creates in the state, county, or city.

The only problem with public sector programs is that they fall under a wide umbrella of agencies that vary in name from state to state. They might be called a micro loan program, a lengthy deposit program, a revolving loan program, GAP financing, or something else entirely. You will have to dig around to find out what they are called in your state or region.

Start with your state's department of economic development and ask if there are any programs that are tied to job creation. Kezios suggests that you explain your purpose to the person you contact and what kind of franchise you are trying to purchase. You have to educate absolutely *everyone* you talk to, she says. They aren't going to understand franchising or the financial blend approach.

Other spots you might look into for information about job creation programs include city chambers of commerce, county development corporations, local or regional offices of the SBA, the state treasurer's office, or the state department of commerce.

Nobody knows all of the places to go for this kind of information, so you have to dig, dig, dig.

One of the benefits of public sector financing as part of your loan package is that it reduces the risk to the banker and makes your equity investment lower. For example, under a normal loan proposal, the bank might finance 75 percent of the total cost, and you are responsible for the remaining 25 percent. When public sector funds are used to cover 40 percent of the loan, the bank's risk is reduced to 50 percent of the total amount, and your equity investment is dropped to 10 percent.

Schmoozing

Small businesses, and in particular, women- and minority-owned businesses, are the final frontier of banking. It is an untapped market. To help open the frontier, think in terms of developing a relationship with your banker. There is more to doing business with a lender than can be shown by even the most detailed business plan.

Some banking decisions are objective; others are subjective. There has to be a certain personal chemistry to help that relationship along in its early stage.

After you get your loan, don't just walk through the bank, make your deposits, pay your taxes, and walk out. Stop and talk to the loan officers and members of the management team. They say, "Who is that? Oh, that's so and so. She has a such and such business. She's a good person to deal with." Let them get to know you and your business. When you have to meet with that lender for a loan (business or personal), he or she will know you outside of the loan request.

Loan criteria

Even though we covered the seven "Cs" that bankers apply to every loan request, it might be worth looking at them again in the context of this chapter.

Every loan application is considered with the following things in mind:

Character and Strength of Management. Character is the essence of yourself and what you stand for. This is one of those subjective things that lenders look for. How do they test for character? It may be as simple as asking you a question to see if you are vague in your response. It may be that they check your banking history to see that you've had no overdrafts for the past 2 to 3 years, or that you don't live above your means.

If you have a lousy credit situation, let the banker know up front in your first meeting. Your lender *will* give you high marks in the character area if he or she is told *all* the good and bad news right away. Good character gives trust a foundation on which to grow.

Strength of management means work history, education, and depth of management in the current field. It also includes the succession of management. What happens if the bank makes you a loan and something happens to you? Who will run the company and pay back the loan?

Capital Injection.   How much of the company do you own? What is your net worth? Many banks define net worth as 1.5 times the amount of money you are borrowing. For example, if you need a $30,000 loan, the bank wants to see a net worth of $45,000—prior to the loan—including what you're putting into the deal.

Capacity to Earn.   Is there a growing, viable market for this business? This is typically addressed in the narrative of the business plan with financial implications laid out in the historical and projected financial statements. Is there enough of a market for you to sell your product at the retail level?

Cash Flow.   The primary source of repayment of the loan is your cash flow. Can the business repay the debt out of its cash flow? If not, what are the alternative methods of repayment? Alternative sources of repayment are secondary to a lender—they don't want to liquidate your equipment or sell off your inventory.

Banks do finance working capital to help with cash flow. But *don't* go in saying, "I want to finance my payroll." Say, "I want help with my cash flow."

Conditions of the Marketplace.   Is the market saturated? For example, some lenders are *not* interested in retail video stores nowadays. Others don't finance restaurant chains. An important condition of the marketplace is your competition.

Current Credit Rating.   This applies to both business and personal credit rating. These are the tangible tracks from the past.

Credit cards in your own name are important if you don't already have them.

Collateral.   Is the loan well secured by collateral? There has been an effort among state-sponsored finance initiatives to ask participating banks to expand their definition of what might be considered acceptable collateral (traditional versus nontraditional). Many banks are now including accounts receivables, government receivables, signed government and private sector contracts, purchase orders, collection/payment records, among others, as acceptable forms of collateral.

9
When one isn't enough

You may look at all of this and decide that having a single franchise is small potatoes. For certain kinds of entrepreneurs, more challenge and more reward is intriguing, even necessary. But even if you are that type, you might want the advantages of working with a partner who has done the work in a particular industry that suggests the franchise is going to be a success.

You might also be a successful franchisee who has a strong belief in the system, and who wants to be in on the ground floor of strong growth. For you, there is the opportunity to work with a franchisor who is interested in rapid expansion by becoming a developer of many units, either as an area developer or a master franchisor (also called a subfranchisor).

In the last three chapters, we looked at the typical sources of financing available to the single-unit franchisee. Except in the cases of larger projects, such as hotels or restaurants, most single-unit franchisees look to personal savings, family, local banks, and government programs as the source of capital to develop their franchised business.

When a franchisee commits to develop multiple units, however, whether as an area developer or as a subfranchisor, its financial needs are greater and require more sophisticated methods of raising capital. The multi-unit developer typically will have the potential to offer the venture capitalist the traditional ranges of return on investment they expect, or will usually be seeking to raise enough money to make the costs of a private placement worthwhile.

Before we go into the specifics of each method for raising capital, let's take a look at the structure and negotiation of area development agreements and subfranchising agreements in greater detail.

Area development and subfranchising agreements

There are two primary types of multi-unit developers: subfranchisors and area developers. Subfranchisors, or master franchisees, act as independent selling organizations that are responsible for recruiting and supporting franchisees within their given region. In certain cases, subfranchisors are allowed to open their own units within the designated territory. Area developers are not granted rights of resale and have no direct support responsibilities, but they are responsible for meeting a mandatory schedule for developing units within their given region.

There are a wide variety of variations on these two principal types of multi-unit developers. For example, some franchise relationships that are at the inception single-unit franchisees evolve to include multiple-unit owners through the use of option agreements or rights of first refusal. Other franchisors have experimented with codevelopment rights among adjacent franchisees of nearby territories, franchises coupled with management agreements (under those circumstances where the franchisee deserves to be more passive), equity participation by franchisors in franchisees (and vice versa), employee ownership of franchisor-operated units, and codevelopment rights between the franchisor and franchisee.

Understanding and negotiating area development agreements

If you want to become an area developer, you will need to discuss with the franchisor the size of the territory, the fee structure, and the mandatory timetable for development and ownership of the units. Bear in mind that the franchisor will usually want to reserve certain rights and remedies in the event that you default on your development obligations. You may be obligated to develop from 3 to 30 units, depending on your financial resources.

You must usually pay an umbrella development fee for the region, over and above the individual initial fee that will be due as each unit becomes operational within your territory. The amount of the fee will vary, depending on factors such as the strength of the franchisor's trademarks and market share, the size of the territory, and the term (and renewal) of the agreement. The fee is essentially a payment to the franchisor that prevents the franchisor from offering any other franchises within your region (unless you default).

Understanding and negotiating subfranchising agreements

Subfranchise agreements present a myriad of complex issues that are not raised in the sale of a single-unit franchise or an area development agreement. This is primarily because the rewards and responsibilities of the subfranchisor are much different than the area developer or single-unit operator.

In most subfranchising relationships, the franchisor shares a portion of the initial franchise fee and ongoing royalty fees with the subfranchisor in exchange for the subfranchisor's assuming responsibilities within the region. The proportions in which fees are shared usually have a direct relationship to the exact responsibilities of the subfranchisor. For example, if you are primarily responsible for all phases of initial and ongoing support of the franchisees in your region, then you should expect to collect the lion's share of the initial franchise fees and ongoing royalty fees. If responsibilities are to be shared more equally, then the fee-sharing should be adjusted accordingly.

The franchisor should provide you with a training program and a comprehensive regional operations manual that covers sales and promotions, training and field support, and related matters over and above the information contained in the operations manuals provided to individual franchisees.

There are a number of questions you have to ask during the negotiation for a subfranchising agreement, including:

1. How will the initial and ongoing franchise fees be divided among franchisor and subfranchisor? Who will be responsible for the collection and processing of franchise fees?
2. Will the subfranchisor be a party to the individual franchise agreements, or will the agreements be limited to the franchisor and the individual franchisee?
3. What is the exact nature of the subfranchisor's recruitment, site selection, franchising, and training policies and ongoing support to the individual franchisees within its region?
4. Who will be responsible for the preparation and filing of franchise offering documents in the those states where the subfranchisor must file separately?

5. What mandatory development schedules and related performance quotas will be imposed on the subfranchisor?

6. Will the subfranchisor be granted the rights to operate individual units within the territory? If so, how will these units be priced?

7. How much must the subfranchisor initially pay to the franchisor for the exclusive rights to develop the territory?

8. What rights of approval will the franchisor retain with respect to the sale and marketing of individual franchises (background of the potential franchisee, use of approved marketing and peripheral materials, approval of local advertising, any negotiated changes in the agreement, decision to terminate, etc.)?

9. What rights does the franchisor reserve to modify the size of the territory or repurchase it from the subfranchisor?

A subfranchisor enters into what is typically referred to as a regional development agreement with the franchisor. This agreement grants the subfranchisor rights to develop a particular region. The regional development agreement is not a franchise agreement to operate any individual franchise units. It grants the subfranchisor the right to sell franchises to individuals using the franchisor's system and proprietary marks solely for the purpose of recruitment, management, supervision, and support of individual franchisees. To the extent that the subfranchisor itself directly develops units, then an individual franchise agreement for each unit is required.

So how do we get these big bucks?

The capital requirements for an area developer or subfranchisor are larger and more complex than for a typical single-unit franchisee. The area developer needs large pools of capital to construct and open units in accordance with the development schedule. Although certain equipment can be leased, many expenses will require equity capital.

The subfranchisor, too, needs to raise capital in order to pay for certain "soft costs," such as for hiring sales personnel, developing a marketing program, and placing advertisements. These costs are also candidates for equity financing because banks will not usually lend money for costs not associated with "hard assets," such as equipment or inventory.

There are two primary ways to raise equity capital: private placements and venture capital.

And as with any business, you need to have a well-written business plan before even thinking about trying to find the money. You will certainly want to work with a law firm to prepare a private placement, or with a venture capital firm if you want their support. In both cases, however, business plans float across the desk in large numbers, so yours must stand out.

Outline of a typical business plan

I. Executive Summary

This section is an overview of the franchise rights being acquired, the business format of the franchisor, the key terms of the master license or area development agreement, the amount of capital required, and your plan for operating and managing the business. You generally write the executive summary after the rest of the plan, but you may write it first and then revise it (many times).

II. Introduction

A. A description of the unique features of the franchisor's business format and the principal products or services that you will offer.

B. A summary of how and why your business will successfully compete with other franchised and nonfranchised operations.

III. Management Team

A. An organization chart and a list of responsibilities.

B. A list of key management personnel and their backgrounds. This is an important part of your plan because the credibility of the team is essential to getting money of any kind.

C. A description of professional support (noting the strengths and background of your attorneys, accountants, consultants, advertising agency, bank, and service organizations).

IV. Financial plan

A. The amount and type of capital required and a plan of allocation.

B. A projected balance sheet and income and cash flow statements for the first 3 years (projections should be provided for the first year on a monthly basis).

C. Assumptions and explanatory footnotes (include historic data in this section).

V. Territory

    A. A description of the designated territory.

    B. Market demographics for the designated territory (as they apply to both prospective customers and prospective franchisees).

    C. General population trends (population per square mile, age, ethnic origin; number and size of families; number of single homes/apartments; average income level; education level; number employed and unemployed; retail spending habits; etc.).

VI. Market Research and Analysis

    A. Customers/prospective franchises.

      1. Who and where are your major customers? How will you attract and keep customers?

      2. What are the key factors that influence their purchasing decisions (i.e., price, quality, service)?

      3. What are the characteristics of your typical franchisee? If you are a subfranchisor, what methods will be employed to attract this target candidate?

    B. Competition.

      1. Identify the key competitors in your market for both customer and prospective franchisees.

      2. Discuss the strengths and weaknesses of each of your key competitors and their products or services.

    C. The industry.

      1. Define the scope of your industry.

      2. Describe the current status and size of your industry.

      3. List major current and likely future trends in the industry.

VII. Analysis of the Franchisor

    A. What is the experience level of the franchisor's management team?

    B. What is their track record? How long has the franchisor been in business, both as a company and as a franchisor?

    C. Does the franchisor have a good reputation for quality, service, and fairness? Have you spoken to other franchisees? Are they happy? Profitable?

    D. How many new franchises does the company intend to award during the next 12 months, 3 years, 5 years? Is the company growing too fast or too slow? Why?

    E. Has the company been involved in any legal action

against its franchisees or vice versa? Are there any suits pending?

F. What is the company's current financial condition?

VIII. Analysis of the Master License or Area Development Agreement

A. What is the term of the agreement?

B. What are the conditions for renewal? Are there any fees payable at the renewal date?

C. What are the provisions for the protection of your territory? Are there any special conditions?

D. What are the initial and ongoing fees and cash requirements?

E. Under what conditions may the agreement be canceled or terminated? Do you have a right to cure? Is it reasonable?

IX. Exhibits to the Business Plan

A. Biographies of the management team.

B. News and promotional information about the franchisor, the industry, or your team.

C. Pictures of sample products, sample location, building plans, and so on.

How the private placement works

Now we're going to get into some complex stuff. We'll try to make it as clear as we can, but if you are seriously considering going the private placement route, you need to understand how complicated it can be. Of course, you will have lawyers and accountants to help you through the steps, but you don't want to be led about like a dog on a leash. It's important to have a good general understanding of the ins and outs of a private placement, so try to bear with us.

A private placement may be used as a vehicle to raise money any time a particular security or transaction is exempt from federal registration requirements under the Securities Act of 1933 (we'll get to that in a minute). In order to determine whether a private placement is a sensible strategy for raising capital, multi-unit developers need to make sure they're covered on several counts. They need to have a fundamental understanding of the federal and state securities laws affecting private placements. They need to be familiar with the basic procedural steps that must be taken before trying to undertake a private placement. And, they must have a team of qualified legal and accounting professionals who are familiar with the securities laws to assist in the offering.

The private placement generally costs less than a public stock or securities offering because it is exempt from many of the extensive registration and reporting requirements imposed by federal and state securities laws. The private placement alternative usually can be a more complex and confidential transaction because it typically will be offered to a small number of sophisticated investors. A private placement also permits a more rapid penetration into the capital markets than would a public offering of securities requiring registration with the Securities and Exchange Commission (SEC).

What about this 1933 Act?

Section 5 of the Securities Act of 1933 requires the filing of a registration statement with the SEC prior to the offer to sell any security in interstate commerce, unless an exemption is available under Sections 3 or 4 of the Act. The penalties for failing to register or for disclosing inaccurate or misleading information under Sections 11 and 12 of the 1933 Act are severe.

If a multi-unit developer wants to avoid offering securities to the public, it must make sure its transaction falls within one of the various categories of exemptions available. These include a broad "private offering" exemption, designed for "transaction by issuers not involving any public offering," an intrastate transaction exemption, and a Regulation D exemption, which is the most commonly used. There are three Regulation D exemptions, all with odd names. We'll run through them quickly because they're important to know.

The first is Rule 504, which permits offers and sales of not more than $1 million in securities (provided that no more than $500,000 is offered and sold without registration under state securities laws) during any 12-month period by any issuer that is not subject to the reporting requirements of the Securities and Exchange Act of 1934 and that is not an investment company. Rule 504 places virtually no limit on the number or the type of investors participating in the offering.

The second, Rule 505, allows for the sale of the multi-unit developer's securities to an unlimited number of "accredited investors" and up to 35 nonaccredited investors—regardless of their net worth, income, or sophistication—in an amount not to exceed $5 million in a 12-month period. Many companies select Rule 505 over Rule 504 because its requirements are consistent with many state securities laws.

An accredited investor is any person who falls within one or more of eight categories specified by Rule 501(a), including officers and directors of the entity who have "policymaking" functions, as well as outside investors who have earned $200,000 per year for the last 2 years (or $300,000 for each of the last 2 years in conjunction with a spouse) or whose net worth exceeds $1 million.

You should keep in mind, however, that if one or more of the purchasers is not an accredited investor within one of the eight categories specified above, then a full private placement memorandum must be prepared and delivered to all purchasers. There is an absolute prohibition on advertising and general solicitation for offerings that fall within Rule 505.

The third exemption, Rule 506, is most attractive to multi-unit developers requiring large amounts of capital because it has no maximum dollar limitation. As with Rule 505, the issuer may sell its securities to an unlimited number of accredited investors and up to 35 nonaccredited investors. The primary variation under Rule 506 is that any nonaccredited investor must be a "sophisticated" investor. In this context, a "sophisticated" investor is one who does not fall within any of the eight categories specified by Rule 501(a), but who is believed by the issuer to "have knowledge and experience in financial and business matters that render him capable of evaluating the merits and understanding the risks posed by the transaction, either acting alone or in conjunction with his purchaser representative."

Rule 506 does eliminate the need to prepare and deliver disclosure documents in any specified format if only accredited investors participate in the transaction. The same absolute prohibition on advertising and general solicitation imposed by Rule 505 applies also to Rule 506 offerings.

The state has its say

Full compliance with the federal securities laws is only one level of regulation that must be taken into account when a multi-unit developer is developing plans and strategies to raise capital through an offering of securities. Whether or not the offering is exempt under federal laws, registration may still be required in the states where the securities are to be sold under applicable state securities laws.

Dealing with this maze of regulations is not fun for the developer or his or her legal team. The states have a wide variety of standards of review, ranging from very tough "merit" reviews (designed to ensure that all offerings of securities are fair and equitable) to very lenient "notice only" filings (designed primarily to promote full disclosure). The securities laws of each state where an offer or sale will be made should be checked very carefully prior to the distribution of the offering documents.

What securities might you offer?

There are essentially three types of securities that a multi-unit developer may issue in connection with its private placement: debt securities, equity securities, and hybrid or convertible securities.

Debt securities are usually bonds, notes, or debentures. Typically, a bond is an obligation secured by a mortgage on some property of the company. A debenture or note, however, is unsecured and, therefore, is issued on the strength of the multi-unit developer's reputation, projected earnings, and growth potential.

The terms of the debt security and the yield to the holder will be determined by an evaluation of the level of the risk to the holder and the likelihood of default. For example, debentures usually carry a higher rate of interest because they are unsecured.

Equity securities include common stock, preferred stock, and warrants and options. Each type of equity security carries with it a different set of rights, preferences, and potential rates of return in exchange for the capital contributed to the multi-unit developer. There are three types of equity securities.

A *common stock* offering carries with it a dilution of ownership and is often a traumatic experience for multi-unit area developers who are currently operating as closely held corporations. The need for additional capital for growth, combined with the lack of readily available personal savings or corporate retained earnings, will result in a realignment of the capital structure and a redistribution of ownership and control.

Although the offering of additional common stock is generally costly and entails a surrender of some ownership and control, it does offer the multi-unit area developer an increased equity base and a more secure foundation upon which to build a business while greatly increasing the likelihood of obtaining future debt financing.

Preferred stock has some of the same characteristics as debt securities. For example, a multi-unit area developer who needs to raise additional capital could authorize the issuance of preferred stock, which would carry with it the right to receive dividends at a fixed or even an adjustable rate of return (similar to a loan), with priority over dividends distributed to the holders of the common stock, as well as a preference on the distribution of assets in the event of liquidation.

Preferred stock may or may not have certain rights of voting, convertibility to common stock, antidilution rights, or redemption privileges that may be exercised either by the company or the holder. Although the fixed dividend payments are not tax deductible (as interest payments would be) and ownership of the company is still diluted, there is a balance between risk and reward because the principal invested need not be returned (unless there are provisions for redemption).

In addition, a preferred stockholder's return on investment is limited to a fixed rate (unless there are provisions for convertibility), and the claims of preferred stockholders come after the claims of creditors and bondholders in the event of a failure to pay dividends upon the liquidation of the corporation. The use of convertible preferred stock is especially popular with venture capitalists.

Warrants and options give the holder a right to buy a stated number of shares of common or preferred stock at a specified price and within a specific period of time. If that right is not exercised, it lapses. If the price of the stock rises above the option price, the holder essentially can purchase the stock at a discount, thereby participating in the multi-unit developer's growth.

Convertible securities are similar to warrants and options in that they provide holders with an option to convert their current holdings, upon specified terms and conditions, into common stock of the multi-unit developer. The incentive for conversion is usually the same as for the exercise of a warrant—namely, that the conversion price (i.e., the actual price the company will receive for the common stock when conversion occurs) is more favorable than the rate of return provided by the convertible debenture or preferred stock currently held.

Convertible securities offer several other distinct advantages to a multi-unit developer: (a) an opportunity to sell debt securities at lower interest rates and with less restrictive covenants in exchange for a chance to participate in the company's success if it meets its projections and objectives, (b) a means of generating proceeds 10 to 30 percent above the sale price of common stock at the time the convertible security is issued, (c) a lower dilution in earnings per share, usually because the company can offer fewer shares when convertible securities are offered than in a "straight" debt or equity offering, and (d) a general broadening of the market of prospective purchasers for the company's securities because certain buyers may wish to avoid a direct purchase of common stock and instead consider an investment in convertible securities.

What do you tell investors?

What has to be included in the private placement memorandum (PPM) will vary depending on the size of the offering and nature of the investors under federal securities laws and any applicable state laws. However, there are core elements of a typical private placement memorandum, just as there are for a good business plan.

Introductory Materials.   In order to introduce the prospective investor to the basic terms of the offering, the cover page should include a brief statement about the multi-unit developer and the business format that is being licensed from the franchisor, the terms of the offering (generally in table form), and the precautionary "legends" required by federal and state laws. Legends are certain disclaimers and warnings that must be put in the first few pages of the offering document.

History of the Company.   The first substantive discussion in the PPM should be a statement of the history of the company that will be acquiring the master license or area development rights. This should include a discussion of the principal officers and directors, products and services, management and operating policies, performance history and goals, competition, trends in the industry, advertising and marketing strategy, suppliers and distributors, intellectual property rights, key real and personal property, customer demographics, and any other material information that would be relevant to the investor (such as dependence on a single supplier or availability of a particular raw material). Guess what? You've already done a lot of this for the business plan.

Risk Factors.   The purpose of this section is to outline all of the factors that make the offering or the projected business plans of the multi-unit developer risky or speculative. Naturally, the exact risks to the investors posed by the offering will depend on the nature of the business format being licensed and the trends within the industry.

Capitalization.   The PPM should include a section on the capital structure of the multi-unit developer both before and after the offering, the rights, restrictions and special features of the securities being offered, and any applicable provision of the articles of incorporation or bylaws that affect the multi-unit developer's capitalization, such as preemptive rights, total authorized stock, different classes of shares or restrictions on declaration, and distribution of dividends.

Management of the Company.   The PPM must include a section on the management team. This discussion should include a list of the names, ages, special skills, or characteristics and biographical information on each officer, director, or key consultant; compensation and stock option arrangements; bonus plans; special contracts or arrangements; and any transactions between the company and individual officers and directors that may indicate self-dealing, property acquisitions, including loans, and other related transactions. The role and identity of the multi-unit developer's legal and accounting firms should also be disclosed, as well as any other "expert" retained in connection with the offering.

Terms of the Offering.   This section should describe the terms and conditions of the offering, the number of shares offered and the price; the right of the multi-unit developer to terminate, withdraw, or extend the offering; the right of the franchisor to reject any prospective purchaser; and any arrangements with broker/dealers or other persons or finders in connection with the sale of the securities offered, including commissions to be paid and indemnification arrangements.

Allocation of Proceeds.   The PPM must state the principal purposes for which the net proceeds will be used and the approximate amount intended to be allocated to individual expenditures. Careful thought should be given to this section because failure to use proceeds as described in the PPM could be construed as a materially misleading statement, thereby triggering potential liability on the part of the multi-unit developer and its management team.

Plan of Distribution.   If the securities are to be offered through underwriters, brokers, or dealers (to the extent permitted by federal and state laws), then the names of each "distributor" must be disclosed, as well as the terms and nature of the relationship between the multi-unit developer and each party.

Dilution.   Often promoters and the founders of the multi-unit developer will have acquired their securities at prices substantially below those offered in the PPM. As a result, the book value of shares purchased by prospective investors pursuant to the offering will be substantially diluted. This section should include a discussion of the number of the multi-unit developer's shares that were outstanding prior to the offering, the price paid, the net book value, and the effect on existing shareholders of the proposed offering, as well as dilutive effects on new purchasers at the completion of the offering.

Financial Statements.   The exact financial statements to be provided by the offeror will vary depending on applicable federal and state regulations and the nature and stage of the growth of the business. Special permission may be obtained by the multi-unit developer from the SEC for omission of one or more of the required financial statements as long as investor protection is not compromised. In addition, the multi-unit developer should provide a discussion and explanation of the financial statements and an analysis of the financial condition of the company.

Exhibits.   A multi-unit developer raising capital through a private placement must always keep in mind his or her obligation to provide "all information material to an understanding of the issuer, its business and securities being offered." This means that many of the documents examined by the attorneys and accountants in the due diligence process, such as the articles of incorporation and bylaws of the corporation, key contracts or leases, sample franchise and area development agreements, and résumés of the principals, may be appended as exhibits to the PPM, along with any other nonproprietary information that would be material and relevant to a prospective investor.

The PPM also has to be accompanied by some "subscription materials," of which the principal documents are the *subscription agreement* and the *offeree questionnaire*.

The subscription agreement represents the investor's contractual obligation to buy and the issuer's obligation to sell the securities that are the subject of the offering. The subscription agreement should contain certain representations and warranties by the investor, which serve as evidence of the multi-unit developer's compliance with the applicable federal and state securities laws exemptions.

Offeree questionnaires are designed to elicit information from prospective offerees to establish that they are sophisticated and able to fend for themselves in a Section 4(2) offering. Generally, these questionnaires contain personal information relating to the prospective investor's name, home and business address, telephone numbers, age, social security number, education and employment history, as well as investment and business experience. The requested financial information should include the prospective investor's tax bracket, income, and net worth.

How about venture capital?

We've already run into venture capital when we looked at financing sources for the individual franchise. There it is not a particularly good vehicle, but for the larger multi-unit franchisee, it might well be useful.

Venture capital is used for early financing of new, fast-growing businesses at a relatively high risk. The professional venture capitalist (VC) is usually a highly trained finance professional who manages a pool of venture funds for investment in growing companies on behalf of a group of passive investors.

Multi-unit developers may also take advantage of the small business investment company (SBIC, see Chap. 7). Finally, some private corporations and state governments also manage venture funds for investment in growth companies.

Regardless of the multi-unit developer's particular stage of development, primary products and services, or geographic location, there are several key variables that all venture capital firms consider when analyzing a business plan presented for investment. The presence or absence of these variables ultimately determine whether capital will be committed to the project. These variables generally fall into four categories: the multi-unit developer's management team, products and services, markets, and anticipated return on investment.

Naturally, the VC will be looking for an existing and established franchisor, a multi-unit developer with the experience to properly and aggressively develop the territory, and the potential for very lucrative return on investment. The best place to make your case that your project fits within these guidelines is in the business plan.

Don't just mail the business plan randomly to your local venture capital company. Study the investment criteria of each firm in your region to avoid wasting time and paper by sending a business plan for 65 auto care centers to a firm that specializes in biotechnology investments. And don't send the plan by mail. Try to arrange an introduction or a short meeting with the managing director of the fund.

Tips for negotiating the venture capital transaction

Assuming that the business plan is favorably received by the VC, the multi-unit developer must then assemble a management team that is capable of negotiating the transaction. Most transactions strike a balance between the concerns of the founders of the company, such as dilution of ownership and loss of control, and the concerns of the VC, such as return on investment and a mitigation of business failure risk.

The typical end result of these discussions is a "term sheet" that outlines the key financial and legal terms of the transaction. The term sheet serves as a basis for the negotiation and preparation of the definitive legal documentation. The multi-unit developer should ensure that legal counsel is familiar with the many traps and restrictions that are typically found in venture capital financing documents.

The term sheet may also contain certain rights and obligations of the parties. These may include an obligation to maintain an agreed valuation of the company, an obligation to be responsible for certain costs and expenses in the event the proposed transaction does not take place, or an obligation to secure commitments for financing from additional sources prior to closing.

Negotiations will also take place on the types of securities to be used and the principal terms, conditions, and benefits offered by the securities. The type of securities ultimately selected and the structure of the transaction will usually fall within one of four categories.

Preferred stock is the most typical form of security issued in connection with a venture capital financing. This is because of the many advantages that preferred stock can be structured to offer to an investor, such as convertibility into common stock, dividend and liquidation preferences over the common stock, antidilution protection, mandatory or optional redemption schedules, and special voting rights and preferences.

The convertible debenture is basically a debt instrument (secured or unsecured) that may be converted into equity securities upon specified terms and conditions. Until converted, it offers the VC a fixed rate of return and offers tax advantages (e.g., deductibility of interest payments) to the multi-unit developer. A VC often prefers a convertible debenture in connection with higher-risk transactions because the VC is able to enjoy the elevated position of a creditor until the risk of the company's failure is reduced. Sometimes these instruments are used in connection with bridge financing; the VC expects to convert the debt to equity when the subsequent rounds of capital are raised. Finally, if the debentures are subordinated, commercial lenders will often treat them as the equivalent of an equity security for balance sheet purposes, which enables the multi-unit developer to obtain commercial debt financing.

Debt securities with warrants are often used for the same reasons that convertible debt is used. They protect the VC by putting him or her in the position of a creditor, in return offering a tidy profit in the warrants to purchase common stock at favorable prices and terms. The use of a warrant enables the investor to buy common stock without sacrificing the position as a creditor, as would be the case if only convertible debt was used in the financing.

Common stock is rarely used because "straight" common stock offers the VC no special rights or preferences, no fixed return on investment, no special ability to exercise control over management, and no liquidity to protect against risks. One of the few times that common stock might be selected is when the multi-unit developer wishes to preserve its Subchapter S status under the Internal Revenue Code, which would be jeopardized if a class of preferred stock were to be authorized.

Once the type of security is selected by the multi-unit developer and the VC, steps must be taken to ensure that the authorization and issuance of the security are properly effectuated under applicable state corporate laws. For example, if the multi-unit developer's charter does not provide for a class of preferred stock, then articles of amendment must be prepared, approved by the board of directors and shareholders, and filed with the appropriate state corporation authorities. These articles of amendment will be the focus of negotiation between the multi-unit developer and the VC in terms of voting rights, dividend rates and preferences, mandatory redemption provisions, antidilution protection ("ratchet clauses"), and related special rights and features. If debentures are selected, then negotiations will typically focus on term, interest rate and payment schedule, conversion rights and rates, extent of subordination, remedies for default, acceleration and prepayment rights and underlying security for the instrument, as well as the terms and conditions of any warrants that are granted along with the debentures.

The legal documents involved in a venture capital financing must reflect the end result of the negotiation process between the multi-unit developer and the VC. These documents will contain all of the legal rights and obligations of the parties, striking a balance between the needs and concerns of the multi-unit developer as well as the investment objectives and necessary controls of the VC. These documents generally include a Preferred Stock or Debenture Purchase Agreement ("Investment Agreement"), Stockholders Agreement, Employment and Confidentiality Agreement, Warrant (where applicable), Debenture or Notes (where applicable), Preferred Stock Resolution (to amend the corporate charter, where applicable), Contingent Proxy, Legal Opinion of Company Counsel, and the Registration Rights Agreement. A brief overview of the nature and purposes of some of the key documents follow:

1. *The Investment Agreement.* This document describes all of the material terms and conditions of the financing. It also serves as a type of a disclosure document because certain key historical and financial information is disclosed in the representations and warranties made to the investors. The representations and warranties (along with any exhibits) are designed to provide full disclosure to the investors, which will then provide a basis for evaluating the risk of the investment and structure of the transaction. The Investment Agreement also provides for certain conditions precedent that must be met by the multi-unit developer prior to the closing. These provisions require the company to perform certain acts at or prior to closing as a condition to the investor providing the venture capital financing. The conditions to closing are often used in negotiations to mitigate or eliminate certain risks identified by the investor, such as a class action suit by a group of disgruntled franchisees, but usually they serve as an administrative checklist of actions that must occur at closing.

2. *Stockholders Agreement.* Venture capitalists often require the principal stockholders of the multi-unit developer to become parties to a Stockholders Agreement as a condition to closing on the investment. Any existing stockholders or buy/sell agreements will also be carefully scrutinized and may need to be amended or

terminated as a condition to the investment. The Stockholders Agreement typically contains certain restrictions on the transfer of the company's securities, voting provisions, rights of first refusal and cosale rights in the event of a sale of the founder's securities, antidilution rights, and optional redemption rights for the venture capital investors. For example, the investors may want to reserve a right to purchase additional shares of the franchisor's preferred stock in order to preserve their respective equity ownership in the company in the event that another round of the preferred stock is subsequently issued. This is often accomplished with a contractual preemptive right (as opposed to the right's being contained in the corporate charter, which would make these rights available to all holders of the company's stock).

3. *Employment and Confidentiality Agreements.* Venture capitalists often require key members of the multi-unit developer's management team to execute certain employment and confidentiality agreements as a condition to the investment. These agreements define the obligations of each employee, the compensation package, the grounds for termination, the obligation to preserve and protect the company's intellectual property, and posttermination covenants, such as covenants not to compete or to disclose confidential information.

4. *Registration Rights Agreement.* Many VCs view the eventual public offering of the multi-unit developer's securities pursuant to a registration statement filed with the SEC under the Securities Act of 1933 as the optimal method of achieving investment liquidity and maximum return on investment. As a result, the VC will protect his or her right to participate in the eventual offering with a Registration Rights Agreement. Generally, these registration rights are limited to the multi-unit developer's common stock, which would require the venture capital investors to convert their preferred stock or debentures prior to the time that the registration statement is approved by the SEC. The registration rights may be in the form of "demand rights," which are the investors' right to require the company to prepare, file, and maintain a registration statement, or "piggyback rights," which allow the investors to have their investment securities included in a company-initiated registration. The number of each type of demand or piggyback right, the percentage of investors necessary to exercise these rights, allocation of expenses of registration, the minimum size of the offering, the scope of indemnification, and the selection of underwriters and broker/dealers are all areas of negotiation in the Registration Rights Agreement.

10

Should you buy an existing franchise?

The growing resale market

Franchise owners, like the owners of many other types of small businesses, may suffer from burnout, want to retire, take a job or try a new business opportunity, or even die. For all of these reasons, and then some, a growing "secondary market" is developing for franchised businesses. This is especially true in the 1990s because many small business owners who bought franchises in the 1970s and 1980s are now ready to consider a sale in lieu of a renewal of their franchise rights.

Acquiring an established franchised business presents a different set of acquisition and financing challenges than acquiring a new franchise. First, it's important to know why the franchisee wants to sell the business. Is it due to one of the more common reasons just mentioned, or is it because the unit has been performing poorly? Has the franchisor threatened termination? What steps will you be able to implement to turn around such a business?

Second, you must study the business to find out its true value and to uncover any problems. This process is called *due diligence,* and it is discussed later in this chapter.

Third, you should use the data gathered during the due diligence period to arrive at the final terms, price, and structure of the transaction.

Fourth, you must remember that any transfer of the franchised business will almost certainly require the consent of the franchisor.

The conditions typically set forth as a prerequisite to the approval of this transfer are also discussed later in this chapter.

Finding the right opportunity—the letter of intent

All of the traditional steps discussed in Chaps. 2 and 3 for determining which franchise and franchisor are right for you should be taken before looking at a specific franchise resale opportunity.

But let's suppose that you've decided on a particular franchise, and you're satisfied that it meets all your requirements. You've also had satisfactory discussions with the current franchisee, and you're ready to draw up a *letter of intent*.

The letter of intent is often executed between the buyer and the seller as an agreement in principle to consummate the transaction. Both parties should be very clear as to whether the letter of intent is a binding preliminary contract or merely a memorandum from which the formal legal documents can be drafted once the due diligence is completed.

The letter of intent offers many advantages to both parties, including a psychological commitment to the transaction, a way to expedite the formal negotiations process, and an overview of the matters that require further discussion. You can make a big mistake by being too informal. The letter of intent will commit you and your assets to a long, hard road, and you should impress upon yourself as well as others that you are businesslike and serious.

Should your letter of intent include a price? From the buyer's perspective, the price at which the business should be purchased should not be set until the due diligence has been completed. However, the seller may be hesitant to proceed without a price commitment. Therefore, a range should generally be established with a clause that sets out the factors that will influence the final price. You should always reserve the right to change the price and terms if information that will offset the value of the seller's franchised business is discovered during the due diligence.

It isn't unusual for a seller to request that a buyer execute a confidentiality agreement prior to conducting extensive due diligence in order to protect against finance disclosure of sensitive information if the transaction is not ultimately consummated.

Conducting the due diligence

Once a preliminary agreement has been reached, you and your team of accountants and lawyers should immediately embark on the extensive legal and business due diligence that must occur prior to the closing of the transaction.

The legal due diligence will focus on the potential legal issues and problems that may serve as impediments to the transaction as well as shed light on how the documents should be structured. The business due diligence will focus on the strategic issues surrounding the transaction, such as the status of the relationship with the franchisor and nearby franchisees, the quality of the location, customer and employee relations, and the information necessary for financing the transaction.

Overall, the due diligence process can be tedious, frustrating, time-consuming, and expensive. Yet it is a necessary prerequisite to a well-planned purchase of an existing franchised business, and it can be quite informative and revealing in analyzing the seller's business and in measuring the costs and risks associated with the transaction.

Your seller is going to become defensive, evasive, and impatient during the due diligence phase of the transaction. That's not surprising: Most business owners really don't enjoy having their business operations under a microscope, especially for an extended period of time and by a party searching for skeletons in the closet. Eventually, the seller is likely to give an ultimatum to the prospective buyer: "Finish the due diligence soon or the deal is off."

One way to expedite the due diligence process and ensure that virtually no stone remains unturned is through effective due diligence preparation and planning. The following checklist should be helpful to those considering the purchase of an existing franchised business.

The checklist is written from a legal perspective. Your lawyer should review all legal documents that may be relevant to the structure and pricing of the transaction, indicate the potential legal risks and liabilities to the buyer following the closing, and identify all of the consents and approvals that must be obtained from applicable third parties (such as the franchisor or landlord) and government agencies. Your legal counsel should carefully review the following legal documents and records (where applicable), when analyzing the legal status of the seller of the franchised business.

Corporate (If the Business Is Incorporated)

1. Corporate records of the seller.
   a. Certificate of incorporation and all amendments.
   b. Bylaws as amended.
   c. Minutes books, including resolutions and minutes of all director and shareholder meetings.
   d. List of current shareholders (certified by the corporate secretary) and stock transfer books.
   e. List of all states, countries, and other jurisdictions in which the seller transacts business or is qualified to do business.
   f. Applications or other filings in each state listed in (e), for qualification as a foreign corporation and as evidence of qualification.
2. Agreements among the shareholders.
3. All contracts restricting the sale or transfer of shares of the company, such as buy/sell agreements, subscription agreements, an offeree questionnaire, or contractual rights of first refusal as well as all agreements for the right to purchase shares, such as stock options or warrants.

Financial

1. A list of and copies of management and similar reports or memoranda relating to the material aspects of the business operations or products.
2. Federal, state, and local tax returns and correspondence with federal, state, and local tax officials.
3. Federal filings regarding the Subchapter S status (where applicable) of the seller.
4. Any private placement memorandum prepared and used by the seller (as well as any document used in lieu of a PPM, such as an investment profile or a business plan).
5. Financial statements and other financial reports filed by the seller with the franchisor for the past 5 years, including:
   a. Annual (audited) balance sheets.
   b. Monthly (or other available) balance sheets.
   c. Annual (audited) and monthly (or other available) earnings statements and royalty sales reports.
   d. Annual (audited) and monthly (or other available) statements of advertising contributions.
   e. Notes and material assumptions for all statements described in (a)–(d).

6. Any information or documentation relating to tax assessments, deficiency notices, investigations, audits, or settlement proposals.

Management and Employment

1. All employment agreements.
2. Agreements relating to consulting, management, and financial advisory services and other professional engagements.
3. Copies of all union contracts and collective bargaining agreements.
4. Equal Employment Opportunity Commission (EEOC) and any state equivalent compliance files.
5. Occupational Safety and Health Administration (OSHA) files and records.
6. Employee benefit plans (and copies of literature issued to employees describing such plans), including:
   a. Pension and retirement plans, such as union pension or retirement plans.
   b. Annual reports for pension plans, if any.
   c. Profit-sharing plans.
   d. Stock option plans, including information concerning all options, stock appreciation rights, and other stock-related benefits granted by the company.
   e. Medical and dental plans.
   f. Insurance plans and policies, including:
      (1) Errors and omissions policies.
      (2) Directors' and officers' liability insurance policies.
   g. Any employee stock ownership plan (ESOP) and trust agreement.
   h. Severance pay plans or programs.
   i. All other benefit or incentive plans or arrangements not covered by the foregoing, including welfare benefit plans.
7. All of the seller's personnel policy and procedures manuals.

Tangible and Intangible Assets of the Seller

1. A list of all commitments for rented or leased real and personal property, including location and address, description, terms, options, and annual costs.
2. A list of all real property owned, including location and address, description of general character, and encumbrances.

3. A list of all material tangible assets.
4. A list of all liens on real properties and material tangible assets.
5. Mortgages, deeds, title insurance policies, leases, and other agreements relating to the properties of the seller.
6. Real estate tax bills for the real estate of the seller.

Material Contracts and Obligations of the Seller

1. Copies of all franchise agreements and any addenda, renewals, or updates thereto.
2. Copies of any other agreements between the franchisor and seller pertaining to the management or operation of the franchised business.
3. Documentation relating to all property, liability, and casualty insurance policies owned by the seller, including for each policy a summary description of:
   a. Coverage.
   b. Policy type and number.
   c. Insurer.
   d. Premium.
   e. Expiration date.
   f. Deductible.
   g. Any material changes in any of the foregoing since the inception of the seller.
   h. Claims made under such policies.
4. Contracts for the purchase, sale, or removal of electricity, gas, water, telephone, sewage, power, or any other utility service.
5. Copies of licenses, permits, and governmental approvals applied for or issued to the seller which are required in order to operate the businesses of the seller, such as zoning, operating permits, or health and safety certificates.

Litigation and Claims

1. A list of material litigation or claims for more than $5000 against the seller asserted or threatened with respect to the quality of the products or services sold to customers, including pending or threatened claims.
2. A list of settlement agreements, releases, decrees, orders, or arbitration awards affecting the seller.
3. Documentation regarding correspondence or proceedings with federal, state, or local regulatory agencies.

Structuring the acquisition

There is an almost infinite number of ways in which an acquisition of the seller's business may be structured. There is a wide variety of corporate, tax, and securities law issues that affect the final decision as to the structure of any given transaction. Each issue must be carefully considered from a legal and accounting perspective. However, at the heart of each alternative are the following basic issues:

- Will the buyer be acquiring stock or assets of the seller?
- In what form will the consideration from the buyer to the seller be made (e.g., cash, notes, securities)?
- Will the purchase price be fixed, contingent, or payable over time on an installment basis?
- What are the tax consequences of the proposed structure for the acquisition?

Stock versus asset purchases

Perhaps the most fundamental issue for the seller in structuring the purchase of the franchised business is whether the transaction will take the form of an asset or stock purchase. Each form has its respective advantages and disadvantages, depending on the facts and circumstances surrounding each transaction. You should consider the following factors in determining the ultimate form of the transaction.

Advantages of a Stock Purchase

The business identity, licenses, and permits can usually be preserved.

The corporate identity, contracts, and structure can be continued.

Disadvantages of a Stock Purchase

Less flexibility to "cherry pick" key assets of the seller.

The buyer may be liable for unknown, undisclosed, or contingent liabilities (unless adequately protected in the purchase agreement).

The buyer will be forced to contend with the seller's minority shareholders unless all shares of company are purchased.

Offer and sale of the securities may need to be registered under federal or state securities laws.

Advantages of an Asset Acquisition

The buyer can be selective as to which assets of the seller will be purchased.

The buyer is generally not liable for the seller's liabilities unless specifically assumed under the contract.

Disadvantages of an Asset Acquisition

The bill of sale must be comprehensive (with exhibits attached) in order to ensure that no key assets are overlooked and, as a result, not transferred to the buyer.

A variety of third-party consents will typically be required to transfer key tangible and intangible assets to the buyer.

The seller will be responsible for liquidation of the remaining corporate "shell" and distributing the proceeds of the assets sale to its shareholders, which may result in a double taxation unless a Section 338 election is made.

Asset acquisition requires compliance with applicable state bulk sales statutes, as well as state and local sales and transfer taxes.

Preparing the legal documents

Once the due diligence has been completed, valuations and appraisals have been conducted, terms and price have been initially negotiated, and financing has been arranged, legal counsel must work carefully to structure and begin the preparation of the definitive legal documentation that will memorialize the transaction. An extensive discussion of these documents is beyond the scope of this book; it's important for you to know, however, that the drafting and negotiation process will usually focus on the nature and scope of the seller's representations and warranties, the terms of the seller's indemnification to the buyer, the conditions precedent to closing of the transaction, the responsibilities of the parties during the time period between execution of the purchase agreement and the actual closing, the terms of payment of the purchase price, the scope of postclosing covenants of competition, and any predetermined remedies for breach of the covenants, representations, or warranties.

Managing the transfer process

There is a wide variety of issues and obligations triggered when a current franchisee ("transferor") proposes to sell or transfer its rights under the franchise agreement to a third party ("transferee"), which must always be subject to approval by the franchisor. Some of the key issues in the administration and management of the transfer process are as follows.

1. *Franchisor's right of first refusal.* Many modern-day franchise agreements provide the franchisor with a right of first refusal to essentially match the terms offered by a bona fide third party in the event of a sale or transfer by the franchisee. All of the proper notification, approval, exercise, or waiver procedures set forth in the agreement must be followed.

2. *Data gathering.* Assuming that the franchisor will not be exercising its right of first refusal, the franchisor must begin its due diligence on the proposed transferee. The franchisee and the proposed transferee must be diligent and timely in meeting all information requests of the franchisor in the areas of business experience, financial capability, employment and educational history, and so on. The franchisor should always meet with the prospective transferee for a face-to-face interview.

3. *Document control.* The franchisor should be provided with copies of all correspondence, listings, sales contracts, bulk sales transfer notices, broker agreements and any other paperwork related to the transaction. Providing such documentation will ensure against any misrepresentations, inaccurate earnings claims, or false statements about the franchisor that the transferor may make to the transferee in connection with the proposed transaction. The franchisor should play the role of document reviewer, not document validator. It will be tempting for the transferee to contact the franchisor directly to get its opinions on the fairness of the sales terms, the accuracy of the store's financial performance, or the credibility of the transferee's proposed business plan or pro forma financial statements. Franchisors should help to facilitate the process but resist the temptation of playing a role beyond the review and approval level, unless the franchisor serves as a direct remarketer of the franchise.

4. *Franchise remarketing.* In recent years, some franchisors have become very active in the remarketing of their franchises, essentially serving as a broker for current franchisees who want to sell their businesses. The "secondary market" for franchised businesses continues to flourish as franchising has matured. Many of the franchises initially awarded in the 1970s and early 1980s are now operated by individuals nearing retirement age, and these franchisees are ready to transfer ownership. Franchisors must decide what role they plan to play in this process and what their compensation will be for locating a qualified transferee.

5. *Transfer fees.* The franchisor must devote time and resources to the review and approval of a proposed transfer. Often the franchisor's attorneys must be brought in to review the terms of the proposed transfer. The transferee, once approved, must be trained and supported. All of these costs must be borne by someone, and it is typically not the franchisor. Therefore, the franchise agreement should provide for a transfer fee that is at least enough to cover all of the franchisor's training and administrative costs, which will be incurred in connection with the transfer.

6. *Debt assumption.* A typical condition of the approval of the transfer (discussed on page 127) is that the franchisee pay all of its outstanding financial obligations to the franchisor. In the case of a troubled franchisee, the transferee may be buying the business in exchange for a promissory note, leaving little or no cash for the transferor to pay its debts to the franchisor. If the franchisor is also taking a promissory note back from the transferee, then the terms of the repayment, the security agreements, financing statements, and personal guaranties of both the transferor and transferee must be prepared. Any other defaults by the transferor, which must be cured as a condition to approving the transfer, should be clearly explained to the transferee, especially if any of those defaults will be cured after the consummation of the transfer.

7. *Disclosure of the transferee.* Regardless of specific legal requirements, good franchising practice dictates that the franchisor provide the proposed transferee with a copy of its current disclosure document and clearly explain any new developments, obligations, or problems that may affect the proposed transferee's decision to buy the business and become part of the franchise system. Proposed transferees who are about to become new franchisees do not want to hear about major changes to the franchisor's operating system, class action lawsuits against the franchisor, or the impend-

ing bankruptcy of the franchisor just after they have invested their life savings into the purchase of the business.

8. *Inspection and audit.* The franchisor should always arrange for its field support staff to visit the site of the proposed transfer in order to conduct an inspection and audit. This will give the franchisor insight into any unreported fees owed as well as help determine whether any refurbishment is required as a condition to the approval of the transfer. This is also an opportune time for the franchisor to collect all copies of the operations manual and any other confidential information from the transferor.

9. *Execution of documents.* There is a wide variety of legal documents that may be prepared by the franchisor for execution by the transferor and transferee as a condition to approving the transfer. These documents may include mutual releases, guaranty agreements, representation and acknowledgment letters (for execution by the transferee, which represents their capabilities and acknowledges their undertaking of certain responsibilities, etc.), lease agreements, or consent to sale agreements. There may also be certain "standard" documents that must be executed by the transferee, such as local cooperative advertising participation agreements, sign lease agreements, equipment leases, or inventory purchase agreements.

In addition to the key issues just discussed, a well-drafted franchise agreement should include, at a minimum, the following specific contractual conditions. These conditions must be met prior to the approval of a transfer.

1. All of the franchisee's accrued monetary obligations and all other outstanding obligations to the franchisor, its subsidiaries, affiliates, and suppliers shall be up to date, fully paid, and satisfied.

2. The franchisee shall not be in default of any provision of the agreement, any amendment hereof or successor hereto, any other franchise agreement, or other agreement between the franchisee and the franchisor, or its subsidiaries, affiliates, or suppliers.

3. The franchisee and each of its shareholders, officers, and directors shall have executed a general release, under seal and in a form satisfactory to the franchisor, of any and all claims against the franchisor and its officers, directors, shareholders, and employees in their corporate and indi-

vidual capacities, including, without limitation, claims arising under federal, state, and local laws, rules, and ordinances, provided, however, that the franchisee shall not be required to release the franchisor for violations of federal and state franchise registration and disclosure laws.

4. The transferee shall enter into a written assignment, under seal and in a form satisfactory to the franchisor, assuming and agreeing to discharge all of the franchisee's obligations under this agreement. If the obligations of the franchisee were guaranteed by the transferror, the transferee shall guarantee the performance of all such obligations in writing in a form satisfactory to the franchisor.

5. The transferee shall demonstrate to the franchisor's satisfaction that the transferee meets the franchisor's educational, managerial, and business standards; possesses a good moral character, business reputation, and credit rating; has the aptitude and ability to operate the franchised business herein (as may be evidenced by prior related experience or otherwise); has at least the same managerial and financial criteria required of new franchisees; and shall have sufficient equity capital to operate the franchised business.

6. At the franchisor's option, the transferee shall execute (and/or, upon the franchisor's request, shall cause all interested parties to execute) for a term ending on the expiration date of this agreement and with such renewal term as may be provided by this agreement, the standard form of Franchise Agreement then being offered to new franchisees and such other ancillary agreements as the franchisor may require for the franchised business. These agreements shall supersede this agreement in all respects, and the terms of these agreements may differ from the terms of this agreement, including, without limitation, a higher percentage royalty fee, National Advertising Fund contribution, increase of the minimum local advertising expenditure, and the implementation of additional fees.

7. The transferee shall upgrade, at the transferee's expense, the franchised business to conform to the current specifications then being used in the new franchised businesses, and shall complete the upgrading and other requirements within the time specified by the franchisor.

8. The franchisee shall remain liable for all direct and indirect obligations to the franchisor in connection with the

franchised business prior to the effective date of the transfer, and shall continue to remain responsible for its obligations of nondisclosure, noncompetition, and indemnification as provided elsewhere in this agreement and shall execute any and all instruments reasonably requested by the franchisor to further evidence such liability.

9. At the transferee's expense, the transferee and its manager and employees shall complete any training programs then in effect for current franchisees upon such terms and conditions as the franchisor may reasonably require.

10. The transferee shall have signed an acknowledgment of receipt of all required legal documents, such as the franchise offering circular and the then current franchise agreement and ancillary agreements; and

11. The transferror shall pay to the franchisor a transfer fee equal to _____ percent (____%) of the then current initial franchise fee paid by the new franchisees of the franchisor but in no event shall the said transfer fee exceed _____ dollars ($____) to cover the franchisor's administrative expenses in connection with the proposed transfer.

11
Selling your franchise

If you are reading through this whole book before you begin—and we hope you are—then it's time for us to say that you should think about the end of an enterprise even as you are beginning it.

The time will certainly come when you will need to pass your business on to someone else. You may have started in your late forties, and now you are ready to retire. You may have developed a health problem. You may just want to get at the value you have built up over the years and get back some of the money you have tied up in the franchise.

For some franchisees, no matter how well prepared, the franchise just grows to be too much, or health problems come up, or a family crisis happens, or the franchisees just end up not liking the industry or franchising. Whatever the reason, you need to be prepared for the day you will want to sell.

A good rule of thumb is that you will lose money if you sell your franchise before 3 years of operation; after that you will probably break even or make some money. In the late 1980s, the average time a franchisee held his or her franchise was 4.8 years. Surprised?

When you are selling a franchise, you are in the opposite position as you were in the last chapter. So it's time to look at some of the same issues from the other side. But in this chapter we won't worry as much about the legal issues, as the financial.

When?

Timing is important when it comes to selling any business, and a franchise is no different. Fortunately, the projections for franchised businesses are good, as we saw at the beginning of this book. As far out as anyone can project, the value of the franchise will simply go up.

That doesn't mean that every kind of franchise will do well, so you need to look at the product cycles of your own industry. You might do well to hold on for an extra year or so before putting your business on the market.

Your franchisor should have plenty of advice about selling your business—from timing to valuation to potential buyers. Your first contact should be with the franchisor.

Setting value

A business is a collection of assets with the capability of generating income. When you sell, you're trying to get at the assets, which are then transformed into debt for someone else or replaced with someone else's assets. That means that there has to be generating power to cover the debt someone else must take on, or to make a reasonable return on the investment of assets. Your calculations are designed to ensure a buyer that the income stream will be there.

You also want to know for yourself because you may well become a lender/investor in the new owner by accepting a note for part of the company's value.

Consider what assets you might have:

Building

Building improvements

Leases on the building

Equipment

Leases on equipment

Inventory

Supplies

Licenses in place

Receivables

Contracts with suppliers

Customer lists

Goodwill

You may have all of these things, or you may have only a few. In any case, you have *assets*. That's the object, of course. Your assets are the concrete expression of years of hard work, as well as the assets you tapped to begin the business.

Your object is to turn those assets into cash, or into something that is as good—perhaps an income stream for your retirement. You want someone else to hand over his or her assets or a guarantee of income in exchange for your assets.

As simple as that sounds, the negotiations to bring it about can be quite complex. Begin by looking at all the categories of assets and deductions in Fig. 11-1. When the time comes for you to sell, you need to know what your business is worth and what you will accept for it. This worksheet can help.

There is, too, the inevitable other side of the equation: *debt*. If you have grown your business, perhaps to several units, you may well have borrowed to do so. It's reasonable and prudent, and some of your assets may be committed as collateral.

Here is where your accountant is most useful to you. If you have been operating your business in a sound manner, you should have a number of reports available to you that show the true state of your finances. You should also have that most important of documents, your tax records, which will show your real profit (if you paid taxes, you made money).

From these records, you can place a current value on those things that are exchanged—your leases, annual income (a reasonable projection), inventory, leasehold improvements, and so on.

But wait, you say. Some of those improvements might have been done years before; and they'll be worth more now. This is true, and you'll need to get a reasonable estimate of that. But you also need to take into account that improvements age, or depreciate. And if you've had a good accountant, you will certainly have been taking tax deductions for depreciation over the years. If you get too rambunctious about placing a value on improvements made some time ago, you may have a good deal of that depreciation to recapture—which means you'll owe some taxes. It's also distinctly possible that the improvements are worth less than they were. The company may be upgrading, and the new franchisee may have to make changes and improvements all over again.

It's better to look at the whole value of the building as it now stands. For that purpose, you will need a good appraiser (start with friends and the local chamber of commerce). It's important to have an outside view of the value of the building and its improvements.

If the building is leased, you'll need to look at the value of the leases. Are they transferable? Are they renewable? Are they at better than current rates? If none of that is true, they really aren't worth anything except the time it takes a new owner to negotiate new leases.

```
┌─────────────────────────────────────────────────────────┐
│                      Worksheet                          │
│                                                         │
│  Assets                                                 │
│                                                         │
│    Building                                             │
│                                                         │
│    Building improvements              _____        │
│                                                         │
│    Leases on the building             _____        │
│                                                         │
│    Equipment                          _____        │
│                                                         │
│    Leases on equipment                _____        │
│                                                         │
│    Inventory                          _____        │
│                                                         │
│    Supplies                           _____        │
│                                                         │
│    Licenses in place                  _____        │
│                                                         │
│    Receivables                        _____        │
│                                                         │
│    Contracts with suppliers           _____        │
│                                                         │
│    Customer lists                     _____        │
│                                                         │
│    Goodwill                           _____        │
│                                                         │
│       TOTAL ASSETS                    _____        │
│                                                         │
│  Deductions                           _____        │
│                                                         │
│    Payables                           _____        │
│                                                         │
│    Building depreciation              _____        │
│                                                         │
│    Equipment depreciation             _____        │
│                                                         │
│    Loan balances outstanding          _____        │
│                                                         │
│    Salaries                           _____        │
│                                                         │
│    Taxes due                          _____        │
│                                                         │
│    Other                              _____        │
│                                                         │
│       TOTAL DEDUCTIONS                _____        │
└─────────────────────────────────────────────────────────┘
```

Fig. 11-1   *What's your bottom line?*

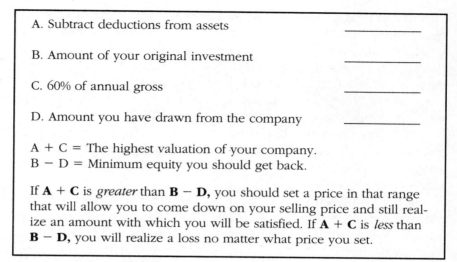

A. Subtract deductions from assets   _____

B. Amount of your original investment   _____

C. 60% of annual gross   _____

D. Amount you have drawn from the company   _____

A + C = The highest valuation of your company.
B − D = Minimum equity you should get back.

If **A** + **C** is *greater* than **B** − **D,** you should set a price in that range that will allow you to come down on your selling price and still realize an amount with which you will be satisfied. If **A** + **C** is *less* than **B** − **D,** you will realize a loss no matter what price you set.

Fig. 11-1   (Continued)

Receivables are not necessarily worth the book value, if they are overdue for some reason. If you habitually allow receivables to run a long time before collection, then you aren't selling a new owner anything of much value.

Finally, you need to be able to give a true profit picture of the previous 5 years in business. Your tax returns are accurate in that they will show your total income. But if you have a good accountant, your tax returns will also be showing as many deductions as possible. You may be deducting for a retirement plan, you'll certainly be taking accelerated depreciation, and there are many perfectly legitimate deductions that may make your actual profit lower than your take-home cash flow.

So you'll need to recalculate to take out the complexities of the tax code for private companies to show what your profit would be if you were maximizing earnings and profits.

What about intangibles?

The hardest part about selling a business is getting others to agree that it's worth what you think it is. In one sense, it's increased in value because of all you've put into it. In another, it's like a used car or house; it isn't worth as much as a new one.

But like any such sale, much depends on perceived value. You need to put together a view of your business that puts its best foot forward. And much of that value comes from those intangibles that you have built up. Those things fall generally into the category of "goodwill"—the perception on the part of customers and vendors that you provide value in your service or product.

A good portion of the value comes from the franchise name that you carry. That is something you have partially built up, but not entirely. The marketing services of your franchisor, not what you have done, have made the franchise nationally significant.

But you do have that name in your location, and nobody else can have it. So it is valuable in that sense—as long as you are going to be able to keep that name (we'll take up this problem a little bit later).

What you need to determine is whether you have built up a customer base that is loyal to you, and whether this customer base will stay with the new owner. You can show this by turning over an up-to-date customer list as evidence that your customers return fairly often. This goodwill is certainly part of your business's assets and a significant part of a franchise.

The value you place on goodwill should be a reasonable estimate of the annual income attributable to repeat business and should go into your final projected income.

You also have a certain amount of expertise with the business that you can offer the new owner. This will help the new owner's transition into the business, and assure him or her that the business will run well after it has been taken over. Your expertise is certainly an asset. It may also help to reassure your customers and make the transition easier for them.

The real number

The most important number is the profit projection for 5 years out. In order to get this number, you have to demonstrate that you've been accurate in budgeting your previous years. You'll need to calculate cash flow, profits, working capital requirements, and balance sheets. From that, you can get a true picture of the cash flow a reasonable businessperson can expect after buying your franchise.

Your buyer (or the buyer's accountant) will look at that projection and figure out what the return would be on his or her investment. If it is a good return—say, more than 25 percent over 5 years—the buyer should be interested.

The projection will help you to set your own price as well. You need to have the return you expect on your own investment. If the return isn't satisfactory to both sides, there will be no deal.

Out of this welter of information will emerge a negotiated price acceptable to everyone. There will be conditions, of course—that you help in a transition for 3 months, for example. Setting a profit projection and determining the value of goodwill based on the projection is difficult for a small business. Often, records aren't kept as they should be, which leads to a problem of credibility.

Don Ervin, a longtime observer of franchising, says that a reasonable formula for most franchise sales is 40 to 60 percent of the gross annual sales. Even if you work out a multiple of net profit of, say, 2.5 to 3 times, it often comes out to the same as 40 to 60 percent of gross. Thus, if your gross sales at your unit have been $400,000, and it is reasonable to expect that to continue, you are looking at a sale price of $160,000 to $240,000. The price might be reduced if equipment has to be replaced or if other improvements have to be made.

How long does it take?

Selling a business can take a long time, but franchises are a bit easier. Their general track record and your specific one will help attract buyers who will feel (as you did) more confident in the business because it is a franchise.

The usual business sale can take between 6 months and 2 years; the franchise sale can take much less. For one thing, your franchisor probably already has a list of qualified buyers who might be prospects for your franchise. Some buyers might particularly want your territory, and that puts you in a very good selling position.

Of course, since the franchisor isn't getting the franchise fee, it may be more interested in steering the qualified buyer in a new direction, but that isn't always the case for a variety of reasons.

Established franchises may be less expensive to buy than a new one at that given point. That's because franchise fees have probably gone up, as have all the related costs—probably faster than the cost of your equity—which could mean that buying an established franchise may be as little as half the cost of a new one. This is especially true of relatively young franchise systems, where the first generation of franchisees is ready to leave the business. If you start with such a young franchise, and its growth is fast, then you might well be in the position of selling your franchise for less than the cost of a new one and still do very well.

Your franchisor might have a buyer whose potential is very good but who just doesn't have the credit to come up with enough to buy the new franchise. Under those circumstances, your franchisor might be happy to have the talents of such a person, who might contribute very well by taking your franchise and continuing to help it grow.

In short, there are plenty of "maybes" in the sale of the franchise. What you need to do is keep clearly in mind what you want to get out of the sale.

A caveat

The sale of the franchise is governed by the initial contract you signed with the franchisor. It may be that you are required to sell your unit back to the company, which will sell it to a new franchisee. It may also be that the term of your contract with the franchisor is running out. If, say, you paid a franchise fee of $20,000 for a term of 20 years and you are selling at 10 years, then the value of the fee remaining is $10,000. If the franchise fee has gone up (as it almost surely has), then in 10 years the new franchisee is looking at coming up with a new, and substantially larger, fee. Your established franchise has to be able to support that increased fee.

Another potential problem is the changes that may have been made in stores by the franchisor. It may be that your location is no longer large enough or that traffic has moved away from it. In those cases, you haven't very much to sell.

Yet another problem is that the franchisor may not be interested in outlets of your size any more or is unwilling to commit to extending the term of the agreement under any circumstances. If, say, your electronics outlet is under pressure from big companies and your franchisor has decided that the only way to go is superstores, your business won't be worth very much—only whatever business can be done in the remaining term of your contract.

In general, however, a good franchisor is not going to stand in your way and will usually help you to make the sale. The important thing to the franchisor is that the franchise unit stays open and keeps generating sales and, therefore, royalties.

Structuring a deal

When the sale time comes, you are going to be in the reverse situation than when you started your business. Now, you have to scrutinize the buyer to make sure the deal will get done.

It is just as unlikely that a buyer will walk up to your door with the requisite asking price in hand as it was that you had the cash in hand when you bought the franchise. For that reason, you may well end up financing part of the sale by taking back some equity or by holding a note for part of the value of the company.

This is not necessarily a bad thing. Granted, you won't have that last $50,000 for a cruise around the world, but then you won't have to count that income for taxes either. (Surely you didn't forget that Uncle Sam will want his piece of the sale?)

In deciding to accept an offer for your business, you should be careful to have the details looked over by your accountant and lawyer, just as you had your original deal examined. You want to make sure the buyer is capable of delivering the down payment and any regular payments you have set up. That means the buyer should be a capable businessperson with some experience running an operation like yours.

Again, you're going to have the help of your franchisor, who will put the new franchisee through the same process it put you through. Once everyone has had a look, you can be reasonably sure that your deal will work.

12
International franchising opportunities

Just as the overwhelming popularity of franchising has captured the attention of the U.S. economy over the past 20 years, the growth of franchising has also skyrocketed in overseas markets. United States–based franchisors are currently operating in more than 160 countries worldwide.

The reasons for this foreign expansion are strikingly similar to the reasons for domestic growth: a greater demand for personal services, higher levels of disposable income, and an increased desire for individual business ownership. Franchisees abroad are responding eagerly to the greater levels of profitability and lower levels of risk, which are inherent in the marketing of an established franchise system.

There are many ways to tap into this exciting international franchising marketplace. The two most typical ways are becoming the master franchisee or area developer in the United States for a foreign franchisor, or relocating to a foreign country to become the master franchisee or area developer for a U.S. concept.

You may have learned about an exciting franchising program in Europe, Asia, or Canada that you feel will work well here in the United States, and more specifically in your region. A wide variety of successful overseas franchisors have found one or more multi-unit developers to penetrate the U.S. market, such as ServiceMaster or Duskin Body Shop.

In such a case, you should be careful that the foreign franchisor has prepared the proper offering documents, has taken steps to protect its trademarks, and that all import laws have been checked if the business format involves the importation of products. Make sure you understand the location and cost of training, as well as the level of support that you can expect from abroad. Also check that all operations and development manuals have been properly translated into American English.

In other words, you have a pretty good model to follow already; if you exercise the same care with a foreign franchisor as you would for a U.S. franchisor, you should be reasonably well protected.

If you are thinking about establishing operations abroad, you run into a host of more complex legal and strategic issues. You need a firm grasp of the culture, laws, markets, economies, and competitors in the targeted country or countries. When subfranchising rights are granted, the master franchisee will need to understand the laws affecting the offer and sale of franchises in the targeted country or countries.

Investigate, investigate, and then look again

What snags are you likely to run into abroad? Some are obvious; some not so easy to catch. Let's look at the major ones.

Language Differences.   All operations and training and marketing materials and manuals must be translated into the local language. Remember that these materials must be understood by your local employees, targeted franchisees, and customers. Not all marketing and promotional campaigns will translate well into the native tongue of the targeted market.

Differences in Tastes.   Franchisors marketing food products have frequently found that foreign tastes differ greatly from American tastes. Make sure that the franchisor makes adjustments to the program and the system before you invest time and money to develop the targeted market. These factors should be carefully reviewed with the assistance of local marketing personnel and product development specialists before undertaking any negotiations with suppliers and distributors.

Changes in Format.   The format and operation of certain types of businesses may need to be modified in certain foreign markets. For example, whereas many overseas markets have developed a taste for "fast food" burgers and hot dogs, differences in culture may dictate that the speed is less important. Customers in other cultures often prefer to relax on the premises after eating a meal rather than taking a meal to go. Sometimes the reasons are cultural; sometimes not. "Take-out" is popular in Tokyo where space is at a premium and consumers are less inclined to expect to linger. The opposite tends to be true in Southern European and Middle Eastern markets, where the pace is slower and the demand for retail space is not as great.

Legal Barriers.   Domestic legislation may not be conducive to establishing franchise and distributorship arrangements. Tax laws, customs laws, import restrictions, corporate organization, and agency/liability laws may all prove to be significant stumbling blocks.

Access to Raw Materials and Human Resources.   Not all countries offer the same open access to critical raw materials and skilled labor that can be found in the United States. Be sure to investigate the availability of these supplies before establishing operations in the targeted market. For example, a chain of steakhouse franchises would be very difficult and expensive to operate in a country experiencing severe meat shortages. Similarly, a tune-up franchisor will run into trouble if there are no skilled auto technicians.

Government Barriers.   The government of the target country may or may not be receptive to foreign investment in general or to franchising in particular. A given country's past history of expropriation, government restrictions, and limitations on currency repatriation may all prove to be decisive factors in determining whether the cost of market penetration is worth the benefits to be potentially derived.

Immigration Laws.   If you are a U.S. citizen seeking to establish master franchising operators in a foreign country, you and your family, as well as any other members of the team you intend to bring with you, must be in compliance with the immigrations laws of the target country.

The law over there, and there, and there

Foreign laws affecting franchising and related distribution programs are changing rapidly. Do not enter into these markets without consulting experienced legal counsel.

That said, we can take a look at how laws are shaking out in major overseas markets—at least in the early 1990s.

European Economic Community. The European Economic Community (EEC), the governing body of the community, was established by the Treaty of Rome in 1957 and now consists of 12 European member states. The six original members—France, Germany, Italy, and the three Benelux countries—were joined by the United Kingdom, Denmark, and Ireland in 1973; by Greece in 1981; and by Spain and Portugal in 1986. The goal of the EEC is to provide a unified internal and external market in goods and services for the member states.

The rules of play governing the EEC's legal system are contained in the Treaty of Rome. Some restraints on trade are not allowed: agreements or concerted practices that directly fix prices, or any other trading conditions that affect interstate trade. In addition, agreements or concerted practices that limit or control supplies or that are designed to share markets are also considered unacceptable.

Quite clearly, the standard franchise arrangement has numerous provisions that would violate these prohibitions. As such, large franchising concerns that operate across EEC borders have had to seek a formal exemption from the Commission.

These exemptions were granted with greater frequency following recent European cases that set the stage for franchising as a legal and legitimate business and expansion practice. Since that time the European Commission has seen fit to establish by regulation a formal "block exemption" setting forth franchising criteria.

The new rules permit clauses requiring the franchisee to refrain from attempting to solicit customers outside its franchised territory, clauses requiring operations to be conducted solely from the franchised premises, and anticompetition clauses that restrict a franchisee's ability to manufacture or sell products competing with the franchisors' products. Other rules allow protection of the franchisor's intellectual property rights, reputation, and common identity of the franchise system.

It's fair to say that without these exemptions and new regulations, franchising could not have made much progress in the European Community. No franchisor would want to risk the kind of cutthroat competition that would have ensued. Without some restrictions, franchisors simply wouldn't touch the markets.

Franchisors are not permitted to prevent franchisees from supplying one another or from obtaining products from other authorized dealers, and franchisors may not restrict the franchisee's determination of prices for goods or services, or prevent former franchisees from utilizing franchise know-how that has become part of the "public domain." These provisions are far more detailed than those in most foreign jurisdictions, and the laws of the individual member states will have to conform to these provisions. Specific provisions have also been established to address "block exemptions" for know-how licensing agreements.

Franchisors entering the EEC should notify the Commission of their intent to do so, referring to the block exemption, and provide details of the contemplated arrangements. If no opposition is lodged by the Commission within 6 months of notification, an official exemption will issue.

A special case: France

France has one of the oldest and largest franchising systems in the European market. Today there are over 600 franchisors and 33,000 franchisees, with franchising accounting for 6 percent of total sales and services in France.

Although France follows the general "block exemption" provisions set forth by the European Commission, it has also implemented the Loi Doubin, a full disclosure rule effective since 1991 which clarifies a franchisor's duties prior to entering a formal agreement with a franchisee.

The law requires that a franchisor, either 20 days before the signing of the contract or 20 days before the payment of any sums of money, provide information (including the following) to a prospective franchisee:

- Description of the franchisor's business
- Description of the franchisor's experience
- Description of the franchisor's supply network and methods of operation
- Description of the present state of the market and prospects for its development
- Size of the franchise network
- Principal contract terms (term, renewal, termination, transfer, area of exclusivity)

Although the full disclosure law, according to the Federation Françoise de la Franchise, has diminished the number of new franchisors, those that do exist are growing, and more successful franchisees are looking for ways they can further invest in franchising.

North America

For many years Canada and Mexico have provided logical areas for initial international expansion by domestic franchisors. Proximity alone makes these markets attractive in terms of supervision of franchisees and a greater likelihood of common product interest.

Mexico in 1990 radically liberalized the current market for franchise development. As a result, Mexico has been a hotbed for international franchising.

In Canada, only the province of Alberta has enacted legislation expressly regulating franchising. The Alberta laws specifically require disclosure and registration of any company that is "trading in franchises." The Alberta Franchises Act is very detailed and requires extensive disclosures of the background not only of the master franchisee, but also of any individual who will be selling the franchise within the province. Detailed audited financial statements are also required for the prior 2 to 3 years of operation.

There are limited exemptions from the Alberta Franchises Act, but these only encompass a very few cases. Any master franchisee considering selling franchises in Alberta should recognize that the entire registration process will be expensive and time-consuming.

The regulation of franchising in provinces other than Alberta (and with the exception of Quebec) is generally governed by Canadian common law. Most provinces have specific legislation governing motor vehicle dealers, which requires registration of dealers and their associated salespersons. In addition, Ontario has a Prepaid Services Act, which affects service businesses dealing in health, fitness, sports, dance, talent development, diet, and similar enterprises. This statute restricts maximum initiation fees and maximum advance payments and limits the length of service contracts to 1 year.

Franchisors in Canada are subject to a wide variety of antitrust provisions, securities regulations, and antifraud provisions, but these are similar to their U.S. counterparts.

Master franchisees operating in Quebec are additionally responsible for complying with French language translation requirements, which dictate that business in the province must be conducted in both English and French. There is, however, some question as to whether the original franchise agreement must be presented in French and English or whether a mere statement in French recognizing that an agreement has been reached to provide an English translation is sufficient. To be on the safe side, it would be advisable to present a French translation at the time that the franchise agreement is executed.

Pacific Rim

Hong Kong, having virtually no restrictions on foreign investment, has been a mecca for foreign capital and products through the years. Although market access is relatively uncomplicated, political changes resulting from the relinquishment of the territory by the British in July 1997 may make certain investors reluctant to embark on substantial projects until after the transition is completed and stabilized.

Singapore, Taiwan, and New Zealand all fall into the category of jurisdictions not specifically regulating franchise activity. Singapore and New Zealand generally view foreign franchising as an acceptable and encouraged source of foreign investment.

Taiwan, on the other hand, until recently encouraged foreign investment primarily in targeted high tech fields, most of which were not businesses susceptible to successful franchising. This attitude has changed as government policies become more liberal. Foreign food franchises have already made inroads into the Taiwanese market.

Australia, Japan, Korea, and the Philippines all regulate franchising. The Australian government, in recognizing a need to improve its overall trading balance and economic performance, appointed a Franchising Task Force to search for ways to satisfy the often conflicting concerns of all parties involved in franchising. In a report to the Australian federal cabinet, the task force recommended a self-regulatory Code of Practice, which would address standard disclosure requirements for franchisors, standards of conduct for both franchisors and franchisees, a uniform alternate dispute resolution procedure, and related matters including education, training, consumer protection, name registration, and stamp duties. How such a code would be implemented has yet to be determined, but one possible scenario involves the creation of a government council to administer the code.

Japan's Law Concerning Development of Middle and Small Scale Retailers (the "Retailers Law") is part of a network of domestic legislation designed to support and encourage the development of small retailers over department stores and supermarkets. The benefits provided by this legislation will frequently assist domestic master franchisees of foreign franchisors.

The Retailers Law encompasses franchises through the definitions of "chain business" and "specific chain business." A chain business (1) involves middle- and small-scale retailers, (2) is based on a standard form agreement, and (3) is engaged in the continuous sale of goods and management assistance. A specific chain business (1) grants trademarks, trade names, or other marks to an applicant for the business, and (2) receives payment by the applicant of a certain amount of money. Those businesses falling within the "specific chain business" definition and who are small or middle-scale retailers may seek designation of their small business plan. Designation will permit the enterprise to participate in investment incentives such as preferential loans and accelerated depreciation on certain depreciable assets.

Prospective franchisees in Japan must be provided with the following information in writing: initial amount of money to be deposited or transferred by the applicant; method of sales of goods or provision of services; extent of management assistance to be rendered; trademarks or any other marks the applicant will be permitted to use; term, renewal, termination, and cancellation of the agreement; name, address, and representatives of the person or corporation operating the specific chain business; date of commencement of the specific chain business; money to be paid periodically by the applicant; and obligation of the applicant with regard to structure, design, or layout of the franchised premises. Franchisors may also register voluntarily with the Japanese Franchise Association, providing additional information to be kept on file for reference by the prospective franchisee.

Until recently, under the Foreign Capital Inducement Law, the Korean government provided a limited list of activities open to foreign investment. Recent amendments now provide for a smaller list of prohibited investment areas, with all others being presumably permissible.

Technology licensing arrangements of all kinds must be approved at the federal level. Prior to mid 1986, a mere trademark license could not be accepted as a royalty bearing "technology inducement agreement." Now a royalty-bearing trademark license agreement may be accepted even without the transfer of technology, if the trademark licensor waives any possible tax exemption. After submission of a technology inducement agreement, the relevant Korean ministry must rule within 20 days or the report is deemed to be accepted as presented. Monopoly regulation, fair trade laws, and foreign exchange control provisions also affect franchisors attempting to operate in Korea.

The Philippines accepts franchising agreements that will promote exports, but not franchise systems that do not transfer technology and have no economic benefits to the country. This applies to foreign investment in general, which is encouraged only to the extent that capital-intensive projects utilizing local labor and substantial amounts of domestic raw materials are promoted.

The former Eastern Bloc

Every entrepreneur in the world is rubbing his or her hands over the prospects in the old Iron Curtain countries. To date, only the largest and most economically stable franchisors have undertaken expansion into these markets given the lack of hard currency and the difficulties in repatriating profits. As the domestic economies build and develop, however, these countries should prove to be an increasingly attractive market.

Master franchisees actively seeking to expand into these markets will find that the U.S. government has developed technical assistance and financing programs to support and encourage this type of investment. Most franchising projects in the former communist countries are being undertaken through joint-venture arrangements, but only the more progressive countries such as Poland and Hungary are being targeted. The principal challenges that arise with respect to proposed master franchising operations include shortages of hard currency, difficulties in repatriation because of the nonconvertibility of currency and general currency controls, lack of necessary infrastructure (e.g., ineffective telephone networks, poor shipping and internal transport links), lack of satisfactory raw material supplies, and difficulties in finding prospective individual franchisees with sufficient entrepreneurial/business background and sufficient cash reserves to cover franchise fees and general start-up costs.

These factors indicate that, at least initially, these markets will be most viable for larger franchisors who have greater flexibility and are able to take a long-term view of profitability. Some larger franchisors are already training prospective franchisees in Hungary. These individuals will make up a new class of business owners in Eastern Europe. Franchising in particular is a viable introduction to the for-profit world for a fledgling free-market economy. Bringing in a viable, working system and providing support, know-how, and training in exchange for a monthly royalty is a positive step for both individuals and the economic infrastructure. The next 5 years will no doubt provide incredible growth in this market. Local enthusiasm, combined with both financial and ideological U.S. government support, will open a huge potential market even for small and growing franchisors.

13
Negotiating commercial loan documents

Commercial loans for any business require a series of steps to bolster the bank's confidence and assure it that you will repay as promised. Banks have developed a variety of loan types to cover different kinds of situations that businesses run into in starting up and operating.

Short-Term Loans.   Ordinarily, franchisees use short-term loans for a specific purpose—to buy inventory for a peak season or to cover a period when customers are in arrears—and lenders expect that the loan will be repaid when the purpose has been served. Short-term loans are usually made in the form of a promissory note payable on demand. The promissory note may be secured by the inventory or accounts receivable that the loan is designed to cover, or it may be unsecured, which means that no collateral is required. A series of short-term loans promptly repaid will establish a relationship with a bank and demonstrate creditworthiness.

Operating Lines of Credit.   A line of credit consists of a specific amount of capital that is made available to the borrower on an "as needed" basis over a specified period of time. A line of credit may be short term (60 to 120 days) or intermediate term (1 to 3 years), renewable or nonrenewable, and at a fixed or fluctuating rate of interest. Prospective franchisees should be especially careful to negotiate ceilings on interest rates to avoid excessive commitment, processing, application, and related up-front fees, and to ensure that repayment schedules will not be an undue strain for the operation of the franchise. Franchisees should also ensure that its obligations to make payments against the line of credit are consistent with its own anticipated cash flow projections.

Intermediate Term Loans.   An intermediate-term loan is usually provided over a 3- to 5-year period to acquire equipment, fixtures, furniture, and supplies; to expand existing facilities; to acquire another business; or for working capital. It is likely that virtually all start-up franchisees will need to secure this type of financing for the construction and opening of the franchised business.

The intermediate-term loan is almost always secured, not only by the assets being purchased with the loan proceeds, but also by other assets of the franchisee such as inventory, accounts receivable, equipment, and real estate that may be available to serve as security.

The intermediate-term loan usually calls for a loan agreement, which typically includes restrictive covenants that govern the operation and management of the franchise during the term of the loan. These restrictive covenants are designed to protect the interests of the lender and ensure that all payments are made on a timely basis—before any dividends, employee bonuses, or noncritical expenses are paid.

Equipment Leasing.   Many start-up franchisees desperately need to use (but not necessarily own) certain key resources to fuel and maintain growth. Equipment leasing offers an attractive route. Monthly lease payments are made in lieu of debt-service payments. There are many forms of equipment leasing. Operating leases are generally shorter in term and include repair and maintenance services. Capital leases are generally longer in term, do not include ancillary services, and virtually transfer ownership to the lessee. A major value for this lease is that you can buy the equipment at the end of the lease term for a song—often a dollar. The lease company does not want the equipment back because it has already depreciated it, and the equipment often has no resale value. But it can certainly still be valuable and functional for you, the owner. Equipment that is technically valueless can still work satisfactorily for years. Lease financing may be obtained from a commercial bank or from a specialized equipment leasing company.

Putting it all together

At certain points in discussing a loan of whatever type, you'll have to make sure your business interests are properly represented. There are, after all, several parties to the transaction: you, the bank, and your franchisor.

Each of you has interests that must be served. The bank wants to look at the interest rate for your loan in comparison to the market rate, the rate it will have to pay for funds, the degree of risk it estimates the transaction will carry, and the cost of administering the loan—plus, of course, its own profit. Unless all these things look favorable to the bank, there will be no loan. Moreover, the commercial lender may insist that the collateral you pledge has a value equal to or greater than the amount of the loan.

You as the borrower will need to prove to the bank and to yourself that you can carry such a note. And the franchisor needs to know that you can cover the loan and make the monthly royalty and advertising payments. If the franchisor is lending you some of the money for the down payment, he or she needs to know that your business will be able to support those additional payments. In general, in this transaction, the franchisor will be "standing second" in terms of claims on the collateral provided for the loan. This means that if you fail to keep up the payments, the franchisor will receive his or her share only after all of the lender's obligations have been met. In other words, the franchisor gets what is left over after the lender has taken what is owed.

For your part, you want to protect as many of your assets as possible, as well as know that you can cover all the payments you are committing yourself to. When it comes to collateral, for example, you should attempt to keep certain assets of the franchise outside of the pledge agreement; you may need them later for collateral for additional loans.

Hard assets are not the only form of collateral you can offer. You could assign lease rights, goodwill, insurance policies, or some franchise rights. These intangible assets, naturally, are valuable—really, essential—assets and should be pledged only when you are sure you can repay.

In return for the loan, you will have to keep the lender apprised of your status, which means your continuing ability to repay the loan. The lender may also require some restrictive covenants to make sure you don't overextend yourself or put your collateral at risk. *Affirmative covenants* encompass the obligations of the borrower (and its subsidiaries, except as otherwise provided) during the period that the loan is outstanding. These may include, among others, a number of required actions.

For example, you may be asked to furnish audited statements of income and expenses and balance sheets quarterly and annually. You may also have to supply any financial statements, reports, and returns that are sent to shareholders or governmental agencies. This may entail allowing the lender to visit your business and look at your books (with reasonable safeguards). Of course, you will be expected to maintain accurate books according to generally accepted accounting principles. The lender will be especially disturbed if you play fast and loose with laws and regulations, or allow your property to go downhill.

Because the property isn't exactly yours while it's pledged as collateral, you'll have to keep up maintenance and insurance on it and on yourself. You will also have to keep up all your financial obligations, including timely payment of debts, taxes, salaries, payables, and so on.

As a consequence of the loan, you're not generally free to do a number of things without the permission of the lender. Many of the actions are negotiable, depending on the kind of financial strength you bring to the transaction. The weaker your position, the more *negative covenants* you'll have to live with. That doesn't mean you won't be able to do any of these things under any circumstances, but that you will have to have written permission from your lender.

You're certainly not likely to be allowed to engage in any unrelated businesses (the lender wants you to focus your full attention on the business that's going to be paying the loan). Nor will you be allowed to take out another loan using the same property as collateral. And it's unlikely that you'll be allowed to take on any new loans or leases without certain conditions.

You'll also find yourself restricted in dealings with your company's stock and dividends, and you'll have to keep the business going at a certain level. Your lender will watch to make sure you aren't paying yourself or other officers too much in salary and benefits.

Except in certain cases where you're dealing with financial instruments that are the same as cash, you will be restricted from serving as a guarantor for anyone else's loans. You won't be able to lend money to anyone else either, or to invest in any business other than your own subsidiaries. Again, the borrower doesn't want you to stretch yourself too thin.

Major financial transactions that will materially change your company will be restricted or forbidden. You won't be allowed to merge with another corporation or to sell or lease your assets, unless you're increasing the assets of your company.

The lender will keep an eye on your capital expenditures

and may even limit the amount you may spend on capital improvements in any given period.

You won't be allowed to use a subsidiary to do things your parent company isn't allowed to do, such as incur debt (other than what usually piles up in the form of receivables).

All of these negative covenants can put a crimp in your ability to grow your company, so consider whether you can handle any of these requirements. Debt is a perfectly legitimate way to increase your leverage, but make sure it does that. In any case, you need to make sure that these agreements will not conflict with your own franchise agreement (your franchisor may want to review your loan agreement to make sure).

Regardless of the actual term of the loan, you should negotiate a right to prepay the principal of the loan without penalty or special repayment charges. Many commercial lenders seek to attach prepayment charges to term loans that have a fixed rate of interest, in order to ensure a minimum rate of return over the projected life of the loan.

Try to keep a lid on a whole series of indirect costs and fees in connection with the debt financing: closing costs, processing fees, filing fees, late charges, attorney's fees, out-of-pocket expense reimbursement (courier, travel, photocopying, etc.), court costs, and auditing or inspection fees.

Another way that commercial lenders earn ancillary revenue on loans is by imposing certain depository restrictions on the borrower, such as a restrictive covenant to maintain a certain deposit balance in the company's operating account or the use of the bank as a depository as a condition to closing on the loan.

The nice part: a commitment

When the loan has been approved by the lender, there will be a commitment letter issued before you get the formal documentation. Fig. 13-1 is a typical commitment letter.

The legal documents

In addition to the commitment letter, there will be a series of documents that are part of the loan and which specify what you are committing yourself to. If you don't get all of the following agreements, it may be because you have a small or simple loan, but the larger the loan, the more you will have.

XYZ CORP.

Date:

Mr. and Mrs. Steven Franchisee
123 Main Street   _____
Anytown, CA 91367

Dear Mr. and Mrs. Franchisee:

Congratulations, you have qualified for the Unbelievably Delicious Ice Cream Store (UDIC) Financing Program funded by XYZ Corp. Franchise Finance ("XYZ"). XYZ will fund your UDIC store in Anytown Shopping Center in the amount of $100,000 as follows:

TYPE OF CONTRACT:	Contractual Sales Agreement
LOAN AMOUNT:	$100,000
TERM:	60 months
PAYMENT FACTOR:	.01720 (Nov.–Jan.)
	.02561 (Feb.–Oct.)
	These rates are firm for 120 days. If funded after that time, the factor may be adjusted.
ADVANCE PAYMENTS:	One at $5,160
MONTHLY PAYMENT:	$1,720 (Nov. through Jan.)
	$2,561 (Feb. through Oct.)

This commitment is subject to conditions being met as outlined in this letter.

During the term of the contract, we require:

You agree that XYZ may discuss your franchise business with the Franchisor, UDIC.

Upon request, you provide your current UDIC financial statements, maintain your equity at a minimum of $50,000, and keep your quick ratio (cash equivalents plus receivables divided by current liabilities) at least .8 to 1. If for any reason these requirements are not met, XYZ has the option to require additional collateral or an infusion of capital.

Prior to Funding, that you have the necessary permits and licenses, etc., to operate in compliance with city, county, and state laws.

To secure XYZ's position with collateral for the $100,000 funding, the following is required prior to funding:

$40,000 pledged to XYZ in the form of stocks, bonds, mutual funds, CDs, real estate, etc.

Fig. 13-1   Sample commitment letter.

*Franchise Agreement Assignment.** This assigns the franchise rights of the UDIC location where the equipment and fixtures are being financed.

Landlord Waiver. This allows XYZ access to the financed equipment and fixtures.

Security Interest in all equipment and fixtures (Uniform Commercial Code, UCC).

Certificate of Insurance verifying a property and casualty insurance policy providing "all risk" physical damage or loss in the amount of $100,000, liability coverage for at least $100,000/$300,000 bodily insurance, and $50,000 property damage naming XYZ as the Loss Payee.

Contractual Sales Agreement, which includes personal guarantees.

*Assignments activated only in the event of a default.

The term of the commitment is for a period of 6 months from the date this letter is signed and the $1000 commitment deposit is made. This $1000 deposit will be held by us and applied to your first payment. If you choose not to execute the contract, the deposit reverts to XYZ.

Steven, as we discussed, the *Interim Funding Option* is offered to assist where the Franchisee wants funds made available during the construction period to pay current bills.

To initiate this option, the following is required.

Promissory Note, for the amount to be funded. Note to be converted to your contract within 180 days from the date you sign this letter or 30 days after the opening of your UDIC, whichever comes first.

Interest is paid every 90 days with the balance due at the time note is converted to contract.

Interest Rate 3 points over_____ Prime.

Request, signed for payment with original invoices.

Fee. There is a $10 charge for each check issued.

We value your business and look forward to a long-term business relationship.

Mr. XYZ Jones
National Account Manager

Expiration date for this commitment letter to be signed is September 5, 19__.

Fig. 13-1 (*Continued*)

The undersigned hereby accepts and approves the foregoing commitment and submits herewith a check for the commitment deposit in the amount of $1000.00.

Mr. and Mrs. Steven Franchisee

_____   _____
Mr. Steven Franchisee   Mrs. Steven Franchisee

Fig. 13-1   (*Continued*)

The Loan Agreement.   The loan agreement (see Appendix E) sets forth all the terms and conditions of the transaction between the lender and the borrower. The key provisions are amount, term, repayment schedules and procedures, special fees, insurance requirements, restrictive covenants, the borrower's representations and warranties (with respect to status, capacity, ability to repay, title to properties, litigation, etc.), events of default, and remedies of the lender in the event of default.

The provisions of the agreement and the implications of the covenants should be reviewed carefully by an experienced attorney and a knowledgeable accountant. The long-term legal and financial impact of the restrictive covenants should be analyzed. The franchisee should negotiate to establish a timetable under which certain covenants will be removed or modified as the company's ability to repay is clearly demonstrated.

Do not rely upon any verbal assurances made by the loan officer that a waiver of a default on a payment or a covenant will subsequently be available. You can't be sure you'll always be dealing with that officer, or that the officer is always going to be authorized by the legal representatives of the bank to make some of those promises. In any case, what is written and signed will always take precedence over any verbal commitment. In any agreement, it is incumbent upon you to know what you are signing; do not get overanxious to affix your name just to get your hands on the money.

The Security Agreement.   The security agreement (see Appendix E) identifies the collateral to be pledged in order to secure the loan. It refers to the terms of the loan agreement as well as the promissory note, especially any restrictions on the use of the collateral and the procedures upon default of the debt obligation. The remedies available to the lender under the security agreement in the event of default range anywhere from selling the collateral at a public auction to taking possession of the collateral and using it for an income-producing activity. The proceeds of any alternative chosen by the lender is principally for repaying the outstanding balance of the loan.

Financing Statement.   The financing document is filed with the state and local corporate and land records management authorities in order to record the interests of the lender in the collateral. It is designed to give notice to other potential creditors of the borrower that they will not be getting first crack at the collateral in case of a default because there is a "senior security interest" in the collateral.

Promissory Note.   This is the actual instrument that serves as evidence of the obligation of the borrower to the lender (see Appendix E). Many of its terms will be included in the more comprehensive loan agreement, such as the interest rate, the length of the term, the repayment schedule, the ability of the borrower to prepay without penalty, the conditions under which the lender may declare an event of default, and the rights and remedies available to the lender upon such default.

Guaranty.   Most start-up franchisees are asked initially to personally execute a guaranty as further security in order to mitigate the risk of the transaction to the lender (see Appendix E). This is especially true if you are borrowing as a corporation and the lender wants to make sure that you will also be personally liable for repayment.

The terms of this guaranty should be carefully reviewed and negotiated, especially with respect to the term of the guaranty, the scope, the rights of the lender in the event of default, and the type of guaranty provided. For example, under certain circumstances, the lender can be forced to exhaust all possible remedies against the borrower (the corporation) before being able to proceed against the guarantor (you, personally), or the lender may be limited to proceed against certain assets of the guarantor. Similarly, the extent of the guaranty could be negotiated such that it is reduced on an annual basis as the company grows stronger and its ability to independently service the debt becomes more evident.

The franchisor

The franchisor also has an interest in your loan agreement, since many of the provisions in a typical franchise agreement could be viewed by the lender as detrimental or inconsistent with its best interests. Regardless of the specific content and format of any given franchise agreement, the issues that may need to be negotiated and the provisions that would need to be modified or waived in such a transaction, which will require the cooperation and support of the franchisor, generally include:

- The lender's access to all reports and correspondence between franchisor and franchisee
- The lender's right to approve any changes or modifications to the franchise agreement or the franchise system
- The lender's right, at its option, to step in and cure any defaults by the franchisee prior to termination
- The lender's exemption from the typical covenants against competition and nondisclosure
- The lender's ability to assign the rights under the franchise agreement and/or to designate a substitute franchisee owner/operator in the event of default, incapacity, or death
- The franchisor's consent to subordinate any of its security interests taken in the assets of the franchisee to the security interests granted to the lender
- The franchisor's waiver of its rights of first refusal upon transfer of the franchise
- The lender's right to assume the lease for the franchised location
- A disclaimer stating that the lender is not a guarantor of the franchisee's obligations and shall not be held responsible for the franchisee's defaults
- A covenant by the franchisor that it will take no action which would jeopardize the funds committed by the lender
- A set of representations and warranties from the franchisor to the lender and the franchisee pertaining to the status of the franchisor and its offering documents

- The lender's access to a representative of the franchisor at all times
- The lender's right to approve the site selected by the franchisee
- The lender's right to approve any equipment, inventory, or related financing offered by the franchisor or its affiliates directly to the franchisee
- The lender's right to attend all or part of the training program offered by the franchisor (at no additional charge)
- The lender's right to attend any audit conducted by the franchisor of the franchisee's financial records
- The lender's right to participate or intervene in any litigation or arbitration, at its option, or at a minimum to be kept informed as to the status of all proceedings

Naturally, many of these provisions will be of concern to the franchisor, and these three-way negotiations can often be frustrating, complex, and time-consuming. The end result of the concessions made by the franchisor are typically set forth in a comfort letter (also known as a standby agreement or a cooperation agreement), such as the one shown in Fig. 13-2.

Such a letter really is a kind of comfort to you and to the lender because it puts a value on the collateral and makes it negotiable.

Franchisors are not unused to such negotiations with lenders, and they will often help with details, and may help you to keep from committing more of your assets than you should. In any case, the larger the amount involved, the more you're going to need some kind of legal counsel to make sure it serves all sides well.

_____ , 19__

BIGTIME NATIONAL BANK, N.A.

_____

_____

Attention: Managers

Dear Manager:

Franchise Agreement
Between UDIC (Franchisor)
and Mr. and Mrs. Steven Franchisee (Franchisee)

We refer to the franchise arrangements between ourselves as Franchisor and Mr. and Mrs. Steven Franchisee as Franchisee and the Franchisee's application to Bigtime National Bank, N.A., for financial assistance. In consideration of your extending credit upon such terms as you may arrange with the Franchisee from time to time, UDIC hereby agrees with you as follows:

1. We will use our best efforts to ensure that the Franchisee operates the franchise business in compliance with its Franchise Agreement with us.
2. We will provide you promptly with copies of all offering documents, franchise agreements, financial statements, and reports prepared by us or for us concerning the Franchisee, the franchise business, or the principals thereof and will disclose to you, on a continuing basis, all material particulars known to us concerning the viability of the franchised business.
3. We hereby subordinate all security interests including purchase-money security interests we now have or may acquire in the future in any of the assets or undertaking of the Franchisee to any security interest that you may now have or may hereafter acquire in the same. We agree further that any security interest you may have in the Franchisee's goods which may have become fixtures shall be prior to any security interest we may have therein regardless of when your security interest attached and that we shall not claim priority over any security interest of yours by reason of any right of distress that we may have or acquire against the Franchisee's goods.
4. If the liabilities of the Franchisee to you and us are at any time guaranteed by the same guarantor or guarantors, we agree that we shall not demand or sue for payment from any such guarantor until the indebtedness of the Franchisee to you has been

Fig. 13-2 Pro forma letter of comfort/buy-back agreement on Unbelievably Delicious Ice Cream (UDIC) store's letterhead.

fully satisfied and that we will hold any payments we receive from such guarantor or guarantors in trust for you and will remit the same promptly to you. We agree further that all security interests we acquire in any assets of any guarantor shall be and are hereby subordinated to any security interest you may now have or acquire in the future therein.

5. It is understood that you may take security for your loan by way of a chattel mortgage, deed of trust, debenture or security agreement, or assignment of inventory which will make it possible to repossess the inventory, fixtures, equipment, and leasehold improvements of the store in the event of a default on the part of the Franchisee.

6. If you are in possession of the Franchisee's inventory, equipment, fixtures, leasehold improvements, or other assets and if you so require, we will purchase the same from you upon notice received from you within 30 days of your taking possession thereof. We will repurchase such inventory or such part thereof which you may tender to us, at a price equal to 100% of the price paid by the Franchisee less an adjustment of 25% for discontinued, obsolete, and shop-worn merchandise and administrative expenses. The foregoing obligation to repurchase is limited to inventory for which we have been paid in full.

7. We will purchase equipment, fixtures, and leasehold improvements at the lower of fair market value or costs, less depreciation at 20% per annum using the reducing balance method; in any case, the maximum price payable by us would be 80% of original cost.

8. In connection with the above, we agree to execute and deliver to you such documents as you may request from time to time in order that our undertakings in this letter may be implemented in accordance with the requirements of applicable law.

This letter of agreement constitutes a binding and enforceable obligation on our part and does not contravene any of our existing documents, bylaws, or any agreements we have entered into. Moreover, we have the ability to cause and hereby agree to cause each corporation affiliated with us to perform covenants of this agreement as though each were a party hereto and to execute in evidence of each corporation's agreement to be so bound such documents as you may require from time to time. This letter of agreement is offered to you in consideration of your extending credit to the Franchisee. To indicate your acceptance hereof, please have both enclosed copies of this letter signed by yourself and return one copy to us.

Fig. 13-2 (*Continued*)

Yours truly,

UDIC STORES, INC.

_____

(Title:)

_____

(Title:)

ACCEPTED by BIGTIME NATIONAL BANK, N.A.

Dated:_____

_____

Manager

_____

Branch

Fig. 13-2   (*Continued*)

14

Case Study:
The Right Way
to Franchise

Making the decision

Steve Lowrey has seen franchising from all sides. He has owned franchises, sold them, and is now part owner of Deck the Walls, a franchisor of art and framing located in major malls. Deck the Walls under Lowrey, John Jones, and Pepper Leavine, has become one of the premier franchise companies in the country. It's not one of the largest—and deliberately. But the company knows what it does well, and it is a model of how franchising ought to work. Because Lowrey is the chief franchise salesperson, he knows about financing a new franchise.

Lowrey was a CPA by training and had worked his way up to the chief financial officer of a friend's company. But like so many of us, he wanted to have a business of his own. He went through much of the investigation steps we have recommended in this book and found a company called FrameIt. Lowrey had always liked art, although he wasn't trained in the field, and was attracted to the idea of a shop that specialized in selling art and in framing.

He bought the franchise for his hometown of Evansville, Indiana, and made a success of it. A year later the franchise name was changed to Deck the Walls.

In a year, Lowrey had opened two more stores, one in Indianapolis and the other in Louisville, Kentucky. Because Deck the Walls requires a large population to serve it, stores had to be fairly far apart. And even though three stores in these widely spaced locations might seem to be a lot for one person to take care of, Lowrey began to feel that his growth was limited. He was thinking about getting into a new business.

The parent company of Deck the Walls at the time was WNS, Inc. (the initials stand for another franchise chain, Wicks 'N' Sticks). The founder of WNS admired Lowrey's salesmanship and management skill, and asked him to come to work for the company as director of operations. That required Lowrey to sell his stores, which he did. All of them are still operating.

Shortly after Lowrey went to headquarters, WNS acquired a chain called Prints 'N' Things, located principally in New Jersey, and converted it to franchises.

"Prints 'N' Things was a 12-year-old chain of 42 stores, with one supervisor for every six stores," Lowrey explains. "They had their own warehouse and distribution center, and it was a well-run operation. But despite that, in the first full year [that] it was owned by individual franchisees, the sales increase was 37 percent. The owner-operator being there gives the TLC and commitment to serving the customer that can't be bought from a hired supervisor at any price." The experience confirmed for Lowrey the value of the franchising method.

In 1986, Lowrey became regional vice president of Deck the Walls, then vice president of WNS. Meantime, he began having feelings that there were problems with Deck the Walls. It had grown very fast, but the franchisees were not happy. The parent company's policy of fast growth was meant to increase the stock value for a public offering. It isn't uncommon, but fast growth does have its problems.

"When you grow that fast, you can't train franchisees in quality manner, and you lower your standards for picking locations and franchisees," says Lowrey. "Fast growth requires you to have a staff of commission salespeople who don't pay attention to quality."

Failing stores and unhappy franchisees in a system that could have been quite good encouraged three employees of WNS to look at a management buy-out. John Jones, Pepper Leavine, and Lowrey got together a proposal for WNS that the company was happy to accept. Part of the agreement required the buy-out and closing of a number of unprofitable franchise locations.

Once that was done, the three new owners set about a program of controlled, quality growth.

With 26 employees at the company's "franchise support center"—it has no headquarters as such—and five in the field, Deck the Walls figures it can support a growth rate of 10 to 20 franchises a year, no more. You might look at those figures to get a sense of how growth relates to support staff for any franchise you are considering. It isn't a hard-and-fast rule, but if you find a franchise company that has 50 people at headquarters and that is adding 100 franchises a year, you should probably do a lot of careful investigation about how much support you will be getting as a franchisee.

Lowrey is the chief salesperson for Deck the Walls now. The company does not use a commission sales force, and that gives Lowrey the freedom to say no to a person he believes would not be a good franchisee for Deck the Walls. And saying no does not have to do always with the financial strength of the potential franchisee.

"For so many years, franchisors were only after bringing in franchisees with money," says Lowrey. "But that isn't enough. You have to consider the long-range relationship you will have with that franchisee." And Lowrey agrees with our assessment of what makes a good franchisee: "Good franchisees are not true entrepreneurs. They want to work for themselves, but they want to be part of a team."

So Lowrey looks for team players. The strategy has worked well for the company, which is now considered one of the very top franchise systems in terms of profitability for units and franchisee satisfaction. Its newer franchisees are more and more likely to be escapees from large companies as they downsize. For example, one is senior vice president of a *Fortune* 500 company; another was the strategic planning vice president of another *Fortune* 500 company.

With that wealth of experience, Lowrey has a lot of advice about financing a franchise.

"At the time I bought my first franchise, WNS was offering financing, which was one of the ways that the company fueled its growth," he says. On the surface, that type of financing looks like a great deal for the company and the franchisee. Unfortunately, it doesn't always work that way.

Because WNS was trying to grow quickly, it did not examine franchisees carefully, and it did not always check that the locations were the best. As a result, franchises started to fail—or at least did not make money. And when they failed, the parent company was left holding leases that were a drain on its resources. When Jones, Lowrey, and Leavine took over Deck the Walls, there were still some unprofitable stores. But that has all changed.

Getting the money

Lowrey's first store was a success. To purchase it, he had to come up with $40,000 in cash and WNS financed $120,000. When he bought his second store, Lowrey went a different route. He sought a Small Business Administration guaranteed loan. He was first turned down by several banks (a prerequisite for the SBA guarantee), and then got the financing. His parents lent him the down payment, and he paid off the loan on the first store with the proceeds in addition to opening the second.

When Lowrey sold his three stores to become director of operations of WNS, two were taken by well-financed buyers who paid off the SBA notes, gave Lowrey what he wanted, and still had enough capital to keep running the stores. The first store Lowrey sold to the manager, Carrie Lynn Dillman, who had worked there for 2 years. Dillman got the down payment from her parents, and because of the store's track record, was able to get bank financing for the rest.

Today these bank financing routes are less available. For this you can thank the excesses of the 1980s, when banks were lending to anyone who could breathe, and no one seemed to care how high the national debt went. Now banks are lending to no one.

Part of the reason is that banks have been burned by bad real estate loans; the other part has to do with the national debt. Because the government pays a high interest rate in order to attract the money it needs to keep operating, banks are able to take in depositors' money through certificates of deposit, on which they pay a fairly low interest (at this writing, 3 percent). Then they buy government bonds at 6 percent or more—the difference provides them with a handsome profit, so why should they lend at any risk at all?

This is not good for those who are looking for bank financing (which is why we went into such detail in Chap. 4 on preparing and presenting a loan proposal). Even an SBA guaranteed loan is not that easy to get, and Lowrey doesn't think it will get better soon. Of the buyers of Deck the Walls franchises in 1992, two had enough cash in hand to set up without any outside financing. Two got local financing from banks (but they were in a strong position financially). The others took out SBA guaranteed loans. (As we noted in Chap. 7, the money doesn't actually come from the SBA; the SBA just guarantees that the loan will be paid—from government funds—if the borrower defaults. You would think that with a guarantee like that banks would be falling all over themselves to lend the money. Think again.)

Lowrey and Deck the Walls work often with SBA guaranteed lenders. What that means is that they help their qualified franchisees with the proposal and help reassure the lender that the investment is sound. Because the relationships are good, the support of the parent franchise company is significant in helping the franchisees get the necessary loans.

Even so, there's plenty of money required up front, Lowrey says. "They want a 25 to 30 percent cash investment. So for our $200,000 store, they look for $50,000 to $60,000 cash down, with the remainder to be financed. But half that $140,000 to $150,000 has to be collateralized with assets that are not store assets." That means you must have a home, car, whatever, with that amount of clear value.

Suppose you have a $350,000 house even in a soft real estate market. You'd think you were home free. Not so. What is your mortgage? If, say, you have a $275,000 mortgage, with $50,000 in it and $25,000 worth of appreciation since you bought the house, the bank won't talk to you. You don't have enough collateral.

These are the facts of life in the 1990s. It may well be that the present administration, which seems interested in stimulating economic growth and investment, will come up with some new tools that will encourage lenders to become more active. There is some evidence of this, but it will require reducing the national debt, having the government stay away from the money markets, and making the lending opportunity look attractive to banks once more.

Not all Deck the Walls franchisees have received financing from banks or the SBA. To come up with the financing, some have used their severance pay, and other have cashed in their 401K retirement plans, which, of course, involves a penalty, but which leaves these franchisees with about $30,000 in working capital—but that's enough. Deck the Walls franchises make money from the start.

Know your franchisor

Here is where it is important for us to stress again how important the parent franchise company is. It is hard to separate the franchise from the way the company does business. Of the approximately 3000 franchise companies doing business in the United States, not even 30 percent of them are sound enough to be able to guarantee that you will make money from the start.

You really need to make sure your franchisor has the same kind of philosophy as Deck the Walls—and, no, you probably won't be able to get a Deck the Walls franchise. The company follows up about 1000 leads a year, interviews perhaps 80 of those people, and sells 15 franchises. Why so much agony, and why is that good?

For one thing, Jones, Lowrey, and Leavine are the owners, and they have seen the unfortunate results of forced growth. Second, they have learned over the years who should be a franchisee, how that franchisee should be chosen, where the locations should be, what sells, and how the franchisee in the field needs to be supported.

"We're not willing to put a franchisee in a compromise situation. Some franchisors are just hoping their people make it, and that's not right. We put together a scenario: the right mall, the right franchisee, the right capital situation."

If the franchisor you are working with isn't careful in the current economic climate, you're going to be left holding the bag. A franchise is not something you buy over the phone and put on a credit card. It is, as we have tried to stress, a relationship that has to support two companies—your store and the parent franchise. So you have to figure how you are going to keep a store going, still pay 5 to 8 percent of your gross as a royalty fee, and make a good living in competition to the independent down the street who doesn't have to pay that royalty.

The franchisor should have the way that works clearly in hand, as Deck the Walls does. For example, the independent art and framing gallery may well have the same or similar inventory. But because Deck the Walls has 200 stores in prime locations, each of which is doing $200,000 gross or more each year, it has the clout to enable its franchisees to purchase supplies at a discount. Typically, that discount will be 12 to 15 percent.

"So, on a $100 purchase [franchisees] save 12 to 15 bucks," Lowrey says. "They pay us 6 percent—6 bucks on that sale—so they're still mathematically ahead before they even get all the support we offer them. But if you can't rationalize how that other layer of the company will make money, then you won't yourself."

The mathematics can be interesting. If both the franchise outlet and the independent gross $200,000 before franchise fees, then the $12,000 the franchisee pays in royalty would seem to put him or her behind. But suppose that $100,000 of that was supplies; the franchisee has already saved the $12,000 or more.

And if the franchisor has a good name, then that value is added to the store when the time comes to sell.

Not all of Deck the Walls' franchisees are doing well, and there are a few who want out. Some of them are left over from the early days and are not in good locations. Others are simply not interested in the business.

"Sometimes you're forced to take the franchise back because [franchisees are] not living up to the agreement. We had to assume leases that WNS had guaranteed. So we'd get somebody who wasn't paying the landlord and was on the hook for it. We put them in default, then run [the franchise] as a company store until it's back on track, and then refranchise to a new operator."

The company tries to help out those who are in bad situations. "If we think it's a bad mall, we just negotiate a buy-out." That does not mean the company makes the franchisee whole; usually it means that the franchisee doesn't have a debt any more. But he or she probably won't get the original investment back—another good reason for investigating carefully.

For those who are simply not interested in the business but who are in a good location, Deck the Walls will often find a buyer. The point is, the better the franchisee does, the better the parent does. That's the point of the franchise system.

"We had three stores that were sold to outsiders in 1992," says Lowrey. "Out of our system of 200 stores we have five or six who want to sell. Typically, these are franchisees who aren't paying attention to the business. In bad cases like that we try to find a buyer and make him understand how poorly the store has been operated.

"We resold one store to a couple that had a 40 percent sales increase in a few months and did well over double the previous year's sales volume in their first full year of operation. The only thing that changed there was the franchisee.

"It is the franchisee who takes coaching, direction, and execution responsibility for the store. If the person is not good, that's a weak link. But changing the operator always works. It is not uncommmon in these situations to see store income double."

It doesn't take a genius to see what a well-run system will do: "We're trying to find mediocre operators and get them out of the system."

Formula for buying a franchise

So financing is a logical result of the partnership created between the franchisor and the franchisee. Lowrey underscores the criteria you should use when you think about buying a franchise, which will make it easier to sell when the time comes.

"The person picking our franchise is the kind of person who [feels] compelled to look at art, though they [aren't] artists or art historians. But they have assets and want to channel themselves into a field dealing with art. This is not the same as a guy who buys a power boat distributor because he likes to water ski."

There is an emotional element to choosing a franchise, but that element has to work with a series of others. Herewith, Lowrey's formula: "First, you need to make sure the franchise can do what you need economically.

"Second, you need to see yourself being in that business every day. How do you feel about saying—at a cocktail party, for example—that you run a hot dog stand, or an art framer, or a postal outlet every day? Could you interact with that kind of customer?

"Third, you need to understand the people who run that franchise. The person who creates a franchise company hires people like himself, so a franchisor takes on a certain culture. One way to think of it is as a job interview. Would you want to go to work for this company? Can you live with this company? If all these things match, then that's the franchise to buy."

When it comes to selling the franchise, you should be on the same terms with your franchisor as Deck the Walls franchisees who want to sell. Going to a business broker will not give you the value you expect or need.

"Business brokers don't understand this kind of business. Buying a franchise is partly emotional. Brokers simply sell the bottom line. And they neglect the value of being part of a well-run chain."

One other thing: Your franchise chain should be growing. That doesn't mean simply adding franchisees—the obvious kind of growth—but adding services and enhancing the value of services that already are being sold. Again, Deck the Walls is looking at an unusual way to do this. It is creating another franchise chain called ArtCetera. It is staying in the art field but creating a small store that sells art-oriented gift items. The twist here is that it will not create internal competition and bad feeling. Whoever already owns the Deck the Walls franchise in a particular mall will get the ArtCetera franchise; no one else will.

The proper role of the franchise parent is to add value. Enough of that, and you can sell your franchise with confidence that your selling price will be plenty higher than your purchase price—and it was making a living for you all that time.

Directory of leading franchise lenders

Here is a sampling of lending institutions, banks, and businesses that offer loans to individuals and investors who are interested in owning franchises.

Allied Lending Corporation
(subsidiary of Allied Capital Corp.)
1666 K Street, NW
Suite 901
Washington, DC 20006
(202) 331-1112

AT&T Capital Corporation
5613 DTC Parkway
Suite 450
Englewood, CO 80111
(303) 741-4144

AT&T Small Business Lending Corporation
44 Whippany Rd.
Morristown, NJ 07962-1983
(201) 397-3000

Bank of Montreal
Personal & Commercial Banking Headquarters
First Canadian Place
18th Floor
Toronto, Ontario M5X 1A1
CANADA
(416) 867-5234

Bell Atlantic TriCon Leasing Corp.
95 North Route 17 South
P.O. Box 907
Paramus, NJ 07653

(800) 678-3278

Brauvin Realty Services, Inc.
150 South Wacker
Suite 3200
Chicago, IL 60606
(312) 443-0922

Capital Funding Services
P.O. Box 424
Waco, TX 76703
(817) 753-3114

CAPTEC Financial Group, Inc.
315 East Eisenhower Parkway
Suite 315
Ann Arbor, MI 48108
(313) 994-5505

Citizens & Southern National Bank
35 Broad St.
Atlanta, GA 30303
(404) 581-5057

CNL Investment Company
400 East South St., Suite 500
Orlando, FL 32801
(800) 522-3863

DiVall Real Estate Corporation
273 Village Mall
Waunakee, WI 53597
(608) 849-6760

El Dorado Bank
SBA Department
17300 East 17th St.
Suite K
Tustin, CA 92680

First Commercial Bank, NADBA/First Commercial Capital
P.O. Box 1960
Seguin, TX 78155
(512) 379-0380

Franchise Funding Corp.
21550 Oxnard St.
Suite 760
Woodland Hills, CA 91367
(800) 475-2003

GE Capital
One West State St.
Suite 201-E
Building A
Geneva, IL 60134
(708) 232-2250

PMC Capital
18301 Biscayne Blvd.
2nd Floor South
North Miami Beach, FL 33160
(305) 933-5858

Gulf American SBL, Inc.
700 West 23rd St.
Suite 100
Panama City, FL 32405
(904) 769-3200

Independence Mortgage, Inc.
3010 LBJ Freeway
Suite 920
Dallas, TX 75234
(214) 247-1776

ITT Small Business Finance Corporation
4355 Ruffin Rd.
Suite 100
San Diego, CA 92123
(619) 569-9981

2055 Craigshire Rd.
Suite 400
St. Louis, MO 63146
(314) 576-0872

445 Douglas Ave.
Suite 2005-21
Altamonte Springs, FL 32714
(407) 862-8188

9730 S. Western Ave.
Suite 335
Evergreen Park, IL 60642
(708) 857-8488

400 Chisholm Pl.
Suite 124
Plano, TX 75075

(214) 578-0080

11100 N.E. 8th St.
Suite 610
Bellevue, WA 98004
(206) 635-7262

One Kendall Square
Suite 2200
Cambridge, MA 02139
(617) 621-7082

2055 Craigshire Rd.
Suite 400
St. Louis, MO 63146
(314) 576-0872

One Woodbridge Center Dr.
Third Floor
Woodbridge, NJ 07095
(908) 636-7272

Denver Place South Tower
999 18th St.
Suite 2330
Denver, CO 80202
(303) 298-1244

4600 Park Rd.
Suite 300
Charlotte, NC 28209
(704) 522-0670

Camelback Arboleda Bldg.
1661 East Camelback Rd.
Suite 250B
Phoenix, AZ 85016
(602) 279-6216

Kanaly Trust Co.
4550 Post Oak Place Dr.
Suite 139
Houston, TX 77027
(713) 626-9483

Major Leasing, Inc./Major Capital Corporation
3230 Peachtree Rd., NE
Atlanta, GA 30305
(404) 233-3300

The Money Store Investment Corporation
15760 Ventura Blvd., Suite 823
Encino, CA 91436
(818) 906-2999 or (800) 877-1722

Maryland Small Business Development Financing Authority
Redwood Tower
217 East Redwood St.,
22nd Floor
Baltimore, MD 21202
(410) 333-4270

Merrill Lynch Business Financial Services
33 West Monroe St.
22nd Floor
Chicago, IL 60603
(312) 269-4440

MetLife Capital Corporation
10900 NE 8th St.
Suite 605
Bellevue, WA 98004
(206) 646-5332

National Cooperative Bank
1401 Eye St., NW
Suite 700
Washington, DC 20005
(202) 336-7700

National Westminster Bank USA
Franchise Finance Unit
592 Fifth Ave.
New York, NY 10036
(212) 602-2842

Pacific Funding Group, Inc.
17782 Cowan Ave.
Suite B
Irvine, CA 92714
(714) 474-1788

Phoenix Leasing, Inc.
2401 Kerner Blvd.
San Rafael, CA 94901
(415) 485-4500

SANWA Business Credit Corporation
One South Wacker Dr.

Suite 3900
Chicago, IL 60606
(312) 782-8080

Schulze & Associates
1701 Lake Ave.
Suite 255
Glenview, IL 60025
(708) 998-4500

Small Business Resources, Inc.
2110 W. 23rd St.
Suite A
Panama City, FL 32405
(904) 785-2128

Stephens Franchise Finance
120 Main St.
2nd Floor
N. Little Rock, AR 72114
(501) 374-6036

Stultz Financial
1420 Bristol St. N.
Suite 230
Newport Beach, CA 92660
(714) 476-8244

International Banks

Bank of Montreal
First Canadian Place
18th Floor
Toronto, Ontario M5X 1A1
CANADA
(416) 867-5234

The Bank of Nova Scotia (Scotiabank)
44 King St. West
Toronto, Ontario M5H 1H1
CANADA
(416) 866-4377

Canadian Imperial Bank of Commerce
Commerce Court Postal Station
Toronto, Ontario M5L 1A2

CANADA
(416) 784-6281

National Westminster Bank, PLC
4th Floor, National House
14 Moorgate
London EC2R 6BS
United Kingdom
011-44-71-7-261666

Royal Bank of Canada
Head Office, 1, Place Ville-Marie
Montreal, Quebec H3C 3A9
CANADA
(514) 874-3102

Appendix B

Directory of franchisors who offer direct financing programs

SOURCE: *The 1993 Franchise Annual* (Info Franchise News, 728 Center St., P.O. Box 550, Lewiston, NY 14092-0550).

A growing number of franchise companies offer direct and indirect financial assistance to franchisees. Following is a partial listing of franchise companies involved in financial support.

Advertising and Business Services

Expressions, The Women's Magazine
P.O. Box 111
Woodland Park, CO 80866
(719) 687-6013

Landex Business Reference Guide
44 Union, #650
Lakewood, CO 80228
(303) 969-8094

Money Mailer
14271 Corporate Dr.
Garden Grove, CA 92643
(800) 624-5371

Mr. Sign Franchise
12 Tomkins Ave.
Jericho, NY 11753-1920
(800) 222-7075

National Bridal Publications, Inc.
303 East Livingston Ave.
Columbus, OH 43215
(614) 224-1992

Nightlife Magazines
5550 Merrick Rd.
Massapequa, NY 11758
(516) 797-0250

Signs to Go
2433 Montgomery Highway
Dothan, AL 36301
(205) 793-3236

Signworld
P.O. Box 370
Kona, HI 96745-0370
(800) 545-2777

TV Times
Box 2487
Chapel Hill, NC 27515
(919) 967-5657

Automobile Rental and Leasing

Air Brook Limousine
115 West Passaic St.
Rochelle Park, NJ 07662
(201) 368-3974

American International Rent a Car Corp.
One Harborside Dr.
Boston, MA 02128
(617) 561-1000

Thrifty Rent-a-Car System, Inc.
P.O. Box 35250
Tulsa, OK 74153
(918) 665-9219

Rent-a-Wreck
6053 West Century Blvd.
Suite 550
Los Angeles, CA 90045
(213) 641-4000

USA Rent a Car
4350 West Cypress St., #750
Tampa, FL 33607
(813) 873-3620

Automotive Lubrication and Tune-Up

All Tune and Lube System, Inc.
407 Headquarters Dr.
Millersville, MD 21108
(301) 987-1011

Grease Monkey
1660 Wynkoop
Suite 1160
Denver, CO 80202
(303) 534-1660

Valvoline Instant Oil Change
P.O. Box 14046
Lexington, KY 40512
(800) 622-6846

SpeeDee Oil Change & Tune-Up
6660 Riverside Dr.
Suite 101
Metairie, LA 70003
(504) 454-3783

Automotive: Muffler Shops

Custom Muffler Service Center
5664 South Transit Rd.
Lockport, NY 14094
(716) 433-1214

Merlin's Magic Muffler and Brake
33 West Higgins Rd.
Suite 2050
South Barrington, IL 60010
(800) 652-9900

Automotive: Products and Services

AAA Auto Repair
Route 1, Box 100E
#1F0079
Tazewell, TN 37752
(615) 626-5806 (ext. 111)

Big 10 Tire Stores
1000 Hillcrest Rd., #304
Mobile, AL 36695
(205) 639-0692

Brake World
5415 N.W. 15th St.
Margate, FL 33068
(305) 973-2810

Dan Hanna Auto Wash
P.O. Box 3736
Portland, OR 97208
(503) 659-0361

Goodyear Tire Center
1144 East Market
Akron, OH 44316
(216) 796-3467

MAACO Auto Painting & Bodyworks
381 Brooks Rd.
King of Prussia, PA 19406
(800) 521-6282

Mobile Auto Systems
P.O. Box 2094
Dublin, CA 94545-6834
(415) 828-2131

Ziebart Tidy Car
1290 East Maple Rd.
Troy, MI 48007-1290
(800) 877-1312

Building Products and Services

Armstrong World Industries
P.O. Box 3001
Lancaster, PA 17604
(717) 397-0611

Classy Closets Etc.
2001 West Alameda Dr.
Tempe, AZ 85282-3101
(602) 967-2200

Decowall
5413 Rhea Ave.
Tarzana, CA 91356
(818) 345-2877

Miracle Method Bathroom Restoration
3732 West Century Blvd.
Suite 6
Inglewood, CA 90303
(800) 444-8827

Ryan Homes, Inc.
100 Ryan Ct.
Dept. 500
Pittsburgh, PA 15205
(412) 276-8000

Burglar and Fire Prevention

Chambers Security Systems
1103 Fredericksburg Rd.
San Antonio, TX 78201
(512) 736-2268

Counter Spy Shop
P.O. Box 427
Rye, NY 10580-0427
(914) 934-8100

Dynamark Security Centers, Inc.
P.O. Box 2068
Leitersburg Pike
Hagerstown, MD 21742-2068
(301) 797-2124

Business Products and Services

Broker One—The Investment Center
1097-C Irongate Ln.
Columbus, OH 43213
(614) 864-1440

Check Care Systems, Inc.
P.O. Box 9636
Columbus, GA 31907
(404) 563-3660

Executrain Corp.
1000 Abernathy Rd.
Suite 400
Atlanta, GA 30328
(404) 396-9200

Fax-9
1609 South Murray Blvd.
Colorado Springs, CO 80916
(719) 380-1133

Mail Vault, Inc.
1251 South Reynolds Rd.
Toledo, OH 43615
(419) 389-1212

Office One
1097 Irongate Lane, #C
Columbus, OH 43213-3252
(614) 864-1440

Proforma, Inc.
4705 Van Epps Rd.
Cleveland, OH 44131
(216) 741-0400

Children's Products and Services

Baby-Tenda Corp.
123 South Belmont
Kansas City, MO 64133
(816) 231-2300

Personalized Books
2953 Ladybird Ln.
Dallas, TX 75220
(214) 353-9999

Cleaning Products and Services

Acoustic Clean
2901 Wayzata Blvd.
Minneapolis, MN 55405
(612) 374-1105

Handyman House Calls, Inc.
640 Northland Rd.
Suite 33
Forest Park, OH 45240
(513) 825-3863

Interclean
12075 East 45th Ave.
Suite 200
Denver, CO 80239
(303) 375-0533

Maid Easy
33 Pratt St.

Glastonbury, CT 06033
(203) 659-2953

Sparkle Wash, Inc.
26851 Richmond Rd.
Cleveland, OH 44146
(216) 464-4212

Employment and Personnel

Division 10 Temps
201 East 66th St., #10C
New York, NY 10021-6464
(212) 557-4900

Labor World
8000 North Federal Highway
Boca Raton, FL 33487
(800) 275-5001

*Food: Convenience Stores, Specialty
Shops, and Supermarkets*

Aprat Mart
5100 Poplar Ave.
Suite 2116
Memphis, TN 38137
(901) 761-3084

In N' Out Food Stores
19215 West Eight Mile Rd.
Detroit, MI 48219
(313) 255-0100

Kelly's Coffee and Fudge Factory
15251 Barranca Parkway
Irvine, CA 92718
(714) 727-3764

White Hen Pantry
660 Industrial Dr.
Elmhurst, IL 60126
(312) 833-3100

Food: Donut, Bakery, and Cookie Shops

The Donut Man
9851 13th Ave. North

Minneapolis, MN 55441
(612) 545-1984

Donut Inn, Inc.
6355 Topanga
Woodland Hills, CA 91367
(800) 766-8002

Pepperidge Farm, Inc.
595 Westport Ave.
Norwalk, CT 06851
(203) 846-7000

Food: Ice Cream and Yogurt

5 & Dine
1600 South Eddy
Box 1981
Grand Island, NE 68802
(308) 382-2752

Baskin-Robbins '31' Ice Cream and Yogurt
31 Baskin Robbins Pl.
Glendale, CA 91201
(800) 638-0310

Ice Cream World
3512 Hamilton Blvd.
Allentown, PA 12103-4587
(407) 533-6668

Malibu Magic Frozen Treats
29 South Main St.
West Hartford, CT 06107
(203) 561-3631

Pied Piper Ice Cream, Inc.
131 Goffle Rd.
Hawthorne, NJ 07506
(201) 423-0655

Food: Restaurants and Quick Service

Arby's, Inc.
6917 Collins Ave.
Miami, FL 33141
(404) 262-2729

Dairy Queen, Karmelkorn Shoppes,
Orange Julius
5701 Green Valley Dr.
Minneapolis, MN 55437
(612) 830-0200

Domino's Pizza, Inc.
30 Frank Lloyd Wright Dr.
P.O. Box 997
Ann Arbor, MI 48106-0997
(313) 668-6055

Hubb's Pub
7738 Industrial Dr.
Melbourne, FL 32904-1631
(407) 631-9022

Manchu Wok
400 Fairway Dr.
Unit 106
Deerfield Beach, FL 33441
(305) 481-9555

Pizza Depot
3722 Wheatsheaf Rd.
Huntington Valley, PA 19006
(215) 947-4853

Some Place Else
1863 Apple Ave.
Muskegon, MI 49442
(616) 728-8495

Greeting Services

Kiddiegram Ltd.
3115 Shadow Walk Ln.
Tucker, GA 30084
(404) 491-8245

Hairstyling and Cosmetics

Giorio's Enterprises, Inc.
142 Mineola Ave.
Roslyn Heights, NY 11577
(516) 621-4970

Health Aids and Services

Body Basics Weight Management Centers
12423 62nd N.
Suite 404
Largo, FL 34643
(800) 822-2611

Formu-3 International, Inc.
4790 Douglas Circle, NW
Canton, OH 44718
(216) 499-3334

Great Earth International Franchising Corp.
175 Lauman Ln.
Hicksville, NY 11801
(516) 822-1230

Inches-a-Weigh Figure Salons
P.O. Box 59346
Birmingham, AL 35259-9346
(205) 879-2639

Tan & Tone Fitness Center
106 West 31st St.
Independence, MO 64055
(816) 254-0805

Laundry and Dry Cleaning

The Appearance Professionals, Inc.
13665 East 42nd St.
Suite H
Independence, MO 64055
(800) 872-7951

Thrifty Clean
1501 South LaCienaga Blvd.
Los Angeles, CA 90035
(213) 655-6160

Lawn, Garden Care, and Florists

Affordable Love, Inc.
7103 Cresswyck Ct.
Wexford, PA 15090
(412) 935-3260

Allen's Flowers & Plants
18500 Sherman Way

Reseda, CA 91355
(818) 996-2605

Living Green
5076 Knollwood Ct.
Santa Rosa, CA 95403
(707) 571-8300

Silk Plants Etc.
1755 Butterfield Rd.
Libertyville, IL 60048
(708) 918-0077

Motels, Hotels, and Campgrounds

Camptown U.S.A.
R.F.D. #2, Box 56
Brimfield, MA 01010
(413) 245-9525

Homewood Suites
3742 Lamar Ave.
Memphis, TN 38195
(901) 362-4242

Midway Motor Lodges
1025 South Moorland Rd.
Brookfield, WI 53005
(414) 782-7411

Photo, Framing, and Art

Cygnus Systems, Inc.
1719 Zartman Rd.
Kokomo, IN 46902
(317) 453-7077

The Frameworks Factory
190 Highway 18
East Brunswick, NJ 08816
(201) 247-2220

Jet Photo Lab
18 Winrock Rd.
Montgomery, IL 60538
(708) 896-1170

One Hour Moto-Photo & Portrait Studios
4444 Lake Center Dr.
Dayton, OH 45426
(513) 854-6686

Printing and Copying Services

BCX Printing Centers
4133 Presidential
Suite #1
Lafayette Hill, PA 19444
(800) 955-5212

The Ink Well
2323 Lake Club Dr.
Columbus, OH 43232
(800) 235-2221

Jack's Copy Center
6903 Atlantic Blvd.
Jacksonville, FL 32211
(904) 721-8074

PIP Printing
27001 Agoura Rd.
Agoura Hills, CA 91301
(800) 421-4634

Retail

American Heritage Shutter, Inc.
2345 Dunn Ave.
Memphis, TN 38114-1186
(901) 743-2800

Ben Franklin Stores, Inc.
500 East North Ave.
Carol Stream, IL 60188
(708) 462-6100

The Drapery Factory
80 Tanforan Ave., Suite 10
South San Francisco, CA 94080
(415) 583-1300

Studio Becker Kitchens
2000 Powell St., Suite 1650
Emeryville, CA 94608
(415) 652-4566

Retail: Clothing and Shoes

T-Shirt Plus
3630 IH-35 South
Waco, TX 76703
(817) 662-5050

Retail: Computer, Electronics, and Video

Silver Screen Video, Inc.
1412-B Baytree Rd.
Box 3724
Valdosta, GA 31602
(912) 242-7577

Sports and Recreation

National Pool and Dart Associates, Inc.
Box 527, #IFD601
Tazewell, TN 37879-0527
(615) 626-5806

Water Treatment

AVI Water Products, Inc.
901 West Hawthorne Ln.
West Chicago, IL 60185
(708) 293-3104

Water Services Technology
2015 South Calhoun St.
P.O. Box 11334
Fort Wayne, IN 46857
(219) 456-7277

Miscellaneous

Aerospace Products USA
Box 5677, #IF0164
Fountain City, TN 37918
(615) 626-5806 (ext. 104)

Caribbean Clear Inc.
220 Executive Center Dr.
Suite 310
Columbia, SC 29210
(803) 750-1000

Hold-a-Hill of America
95 South State St.
Laverkin, UT 84745
(801) 635-3828

Press Box News, Inc.
2600 Columbia Ave.
Lancaster, PA 17603
(717) 291-9649

Appendix C

Directory of women and minority franchise lenders and technical assistance

Association of Small Business Development Centers
1313 Farnam on the Mall, Suite 132
Omaha, NE 68182-0472
(404) 595-2387

Business Assistance Consortium, Inc.
Franchise Financing Program
6600 N.W. 27th Ave.
Miami, FL 33147
(305) 693-3550

Business Consortium Fund
15 West 39th St., 9th Floor
New York, NY 10018
(212) 764-5590

The Combined Fund, Inc.
915 East Hyde Park Blvd.
Chicago, IL 60615
(312) 363-0300

U.S. Department of Commerce Minority Business Development
Agency
Office of Program Development
14th and Constitution, Room 5096
Washington, DC 20230
(202) 377-3237

Franchise Resource Assistance Training Program
Howard University School of Business and Public Administration
Small Business Development Center
2600 Sixth St.
Room 128
Washington, DC 20059
(202) 806-1550

Jacksonville Franchise Development Program Economic
Development Company
128 East Forsyth St., Suite 500
Jacksonville, FL 32202
(904) 630-1914

The Maryland Small Business Development Financing Authority
Equity Participation Investment Authority
217 East Redwood St., Suite 2240
Baltimore, MD 21202
(301) 333-4270

Miami-Dade Franchise Technical Assistance Center of the
Chamber of Commerce
6600 N.W. 27th Ave.
Miami, FL 33147
(305) 693-3550

Midwest Development Corporation Franchise Development
Project
P.O. Box 29405
Cincinnati, OH 45229
(513) 281-7814

The National Association of Investment Companies
1111 14th St., NW
Washington, DC 20005
(202) 289-4336

New York State Minority and Women Revolving Loan Fund of the
Urban Development Corporation
1515 Broadway
New York, NY 10036
(212) 930-0452

Pennsylvania Department of Commerce Minority Business
Development Authority
Forum Building, Room 404
Harrisburg, PA 17120
(717) 783-1128

Shingler-Hollis Investment Group, Inc.
8701 Georgia Ave., Suite 501
Silver Spring, MD 20910
(301) 587-4474

Women in Franchising
53 West Jackson Blvd., Suite 756
Chicago, IL 60604
(312) 431-1467

Compass Rose
20 Moores Rd.
Frazer, PA 19355
(800) 678-7930

United States Department of Commerce
Minority Business Development Centers

MBDA's nationwide network of minority business development
centers (MBDCs) facilitate the formation and expansion of and
generate opportunities for minority-owned firms. The services
include help with accounting, administration, business planning,
inventory control, negotiations, networking, construction contracting and subcontracting, marketing, and the SBA's 8(a) certifi-
cation to participate in minority set-aside contracting opportunities with the federal government.

MBDCs also provide assistance for bonding, bidding, esti-
mating, financing, procurement, international trade, franchising,
acquisitions, mergers, joint ventures, and leveraged buyouts.

The locations of all MBDCs are subject to change. Check
with the MBDC regional office nearest you for updates.

*Atlanta Region (covers Alabama, Florida, Georgia, Kentucky,
Mississippi, North Carolina, South Carolina, and Tennessee)*

MBDA Regional Director
61 S.W. First St., NW
Suite 1930
Atlanta, GA 30308-3516
(404) 730-3300

MBDA Miami District Officer
51 S.W. First Ave.
Room 1314, Box 25
Miami, FL 33130
(305) 536-5054

Atlanta MBDC
75 Piedmont Ave., NE
Suite 256
Atlanta, GA 30303
(405) 586-0973

Augusta MBDC
1394 Laney Walker Blvd.
Augusta, GA 30901
(404) 722-0994

Birmingham MBDC
2100 16th Ave., S.
Suite 304
Birmingham, AL 35205
(205) 930-9254

Charleston MBDC
77 Grove St.
Charleston, SC 29403
(803) 722-3618

Charlotte MBDC
700 East Stonewall St.
Suite 360
Charlotte, NC 28202
(704) 334-7522

Columbia MBDC
2230-B Taylor St.
Columbia, SC 29204
(803) 779-5905

Columbus MBDC
1214 First Ave.
Suite 430
Columbus, GA 31902
(404) 324-4253

Fayetteville MBDC
114-1/2 Anderson St.
Fayetteville, NC 28302
(919) 483-7513

Greenville/Spartanburg MBDC
211 Century Plaza Dr.
Suite 100-D
Greenville, SC 29607

Jackson MBDC
5285 Galaxie St.
Suite A
Jackson, MS 39206
(601) 362-2260

Jacksonville MBDC
218 West Adams
Suite 300
Jacksonville, FL 32202
(904) 353-3826

Louisville MBDC
611 West Main St.
4th Floor
Louisville, KY 40202
(502) 589-6232

Memphis MBDC
5 North Third St.
Suite 2020
Memphis, TN 38103
(901) 527-2298

Miami/Ft. Lauderdale MBDC
1200 N.W. 78th Ave.
Suite 301
Miami, FL 33126
(305) 591-7355

Mobile MBDC
801 Executive Park Dr.
Suite 102
Mobile, AL 36606
(205) 471-5165

Montgomery MBDC
770 South McDonough St.
Suite 209
Montgomery, AL 36104
(205) 834-7598

Nashville MBDC
14 Academy Place
Suite 2
Nashville, TN 37210
(615) 255-0432

Orlando MBDC
132 East Colonial Dr.
Suite 211
Orlando, FL 32801
(407) 422-6234

Raleigh/Durham MBDC
817 New Bern Ave.
Suite 8
Raleigh, NC 27601
(919) 833-6122

Savannah MBDC
31 West Congress St.
Suite 201
Savannah, GA 31401
(912) 236-6708

Tampa/St. Petersburg MBDC
4601 West Kennedy Blvd.
Suite 200
Tampa, FL 33609
(813) 289-8824

West Palm Beach MBDC
2001 Broadway
Suite 301
Riveria Beach, FL 33404
(407) 863-0896

Chicago Region (covers Illinois, Indiana, Iowa, Kansas, Michigan, Minnesota, Missouri, Nebraska, Ohio, and Wisconsin)

MBDA Regional Director
55 East Monroe St.
Suite 1440
Chicago, IL 60603
(312) 353-0182

Chicago 1 MBDC
35 East Wacker Dr.
Suite 922
Chicago, IL 60601
(312) 977-9190

Chicago 2 MBDC
700 One Prudential Plaza
Chicago, IL 60601

Cincinnati MBDC
1821 Summit Rd.
Suite 111
Cincinnati, OH 45237
(513) 689-6000

Cleveland MBDC
601 Lakeside
Suite 335
Cleveland, OH 44114
(216) 664-4150

Dayton MBDC
1818 West 3rd St.
Dayton, OH 45417
(513) 263-6232

Detroit MBDC
26913 North Western Highway
Suite 400
Southfield, MI 48034
(313) 262-1967

Gary MBDC
567 Broadway
Gary, IN 46402
(219) 883-5802

Indianapolis MBDC
4755 Kingsway Dr.
Suite 103
Indianapolis, IN 46205

Kansas City MBDC
1101 Walnut St.
Suite 1600
Kansas City, MO 64106
(816) 471-1520

Milwaukee MBDC
3929 North Humboldt Blvd.
Milwaukee, WI 53212
(414) 332-6268

Minneapolis MBDC
2021 East Hennepin Ave.
Suite LL 35
Minneapolis, MN 55413
(612) 331-5576

St. Louis MBDC
500 Washington Ave.
Suite 1200
St. Louis, MO 63101
(314) 621-6232

Dallas Region (covers Arkansas, Colorado, Louisiana, Montana, New Mexico, North Dakota, Oklahoma, South Dakota, Texas, Utah, and Wyoming)

MBDA Regional Director
1100 Commerce St.
Room 7823
Dallas, TX 75242
(214) 767-8001

Albuquerque MBDC
718 Central Ave., SW
Albuquerque, NM 87102
(505) 843-7114

Austin MBDC
301 North Congress Ave.
Suite 1020
Austin, TX 78701
(512) 476-9700

Baton Rouge MBDC
2036 Wooddale Blvd.
Suite D
Baton Rouge, LA 70806
(504) 924-0186

Brownsville MBDC
2100 Boca Chica Blvd.
Suite 301
Brownsville, TX 78521
(512) 546-3400

Corpus Christi MBDC
3649 Leopard St.
Suite 514
Corpus Christi, TX 78404
(512) 887-7961

Dallas/Fort Worth MBDC
1445 Ross Ave.
Suite 800
Dallas, TX 76202
(214) 855-7373

Denver MBDC
930 West 7th Ave.
Denver, CO 80204
(303) 623-5660

El Paso MBDC
6068 Gateway East
Suite 200

El Paso, TX 79905
(915) 774-0626

Houston MBDC
1200 Smith St.
Suite 2870
Houston, TX 77002
(713) 650-3831

Laredo MBDC
777 Calle Del Norte
No. 2
Laredo, TX 78401
(512) 725-5177

Little Rock MBDC
One Riverfront Place
Suite 415
North Little Rock, AR 72114
(501) 372-7312

Lubbock/Midland-Odessa MBDC
1220 Broadway
Suite 509
Lubbock, TX 79401
(806) 762-623

McAllen MBDC
1701 West Business Highway
Suite 1108
McAllen, TX 78501
(512) 687-5224

New Orleans MBDC
1001 Howard Ave.
Suite 2305
New Orleans, LA 70113
(504) 523-5400

Oklahoma City MBDC
1500 N.E. 4th St.
Suite 101
Oklahoma City, OK 73117
(405) 235-0430

Salt Lake City MBDC
350 East 500 South
Suite 101
Salt Lake City, UT 84111
(801) 328-8181

San Antonio MBDC
UTSA, Hemisphere Park
San Antonio, TX 78205
(512) 224-1945

Shreveport MBDC
820 Jordan St.
Suite 105
Shreveport, LA 71101
(318) 226-4931

Tulsa MBDC
240 East Apache St.
Tulsa, OK 74106
(918) 592-1995

New York Region (covers Connecticut, Maine, Massachusetts, New Hampshire, New Jersey, New York, Puerto Rico, Rhode Island, Vermont, and the Virgin Islands)

MBDA Regional Director
26 Federal Plaza
Room 3720
New York, NY 10278
(212) 264-3262

MBDA Boston District Office
10 Causeway St.
Room 418
Boston, MA 02222
(617) 565-6850

Boston MBDC
985 Commonwealth Ave.
Room 201
Boston, MA 02215
(617) 353-7060

Brooklyn MBDC
16 Court St.
Room 1903
Brooklyn, NY 11201
(718) 522-5880

Buffalo MBDC
570 East Delavan Ave.
Buffalo, NY 14211
(716) 895-2218

Connecticut MBDC
410 Asylum Ave.
Suite 243
Hartford, CT 06103
(203) 246-5371

Manhattan MBDC
51 Madison Ave.
Suite 2212
New York, NY 10010
(212) 779-4360

Mayaguez MBDC
70 West Mendez Vigo
P.O. Box 3146 Marina Station
Mayaguez, PR 00681
(809) 833-7783

Nassau/Suffolk MBDC
150 Broad Hollow Rd.
Suite 304
Melville, NY 11747
(516) 549-5454

New Brunswick MBDC
100 Jersey Ave.
Building D, Suite 3
New Brunswick, NJ 08901
(908) 249-5511

Newark MBDC
60 Park Place
Suite 1404
Newark, NJ 07102
(201) 623-7712

Ponce MBDC
19 Salud St.
Ponce, PR 00731
(809) 840-8100

Queens MBDC
110-29 Horaco Harding Expressway
Corona, NY 11368
(718) 699-2400

Rochester MBDC
350 North St.
Rochester, NY 14605
(716) 232-6120

San Juan MBDC
122 Eleanor Roosevelt Ave.
Halo Rey, PR 00918
(809) 753-8484

Virgin Islands MBDC
81-AB Kronprindsen Gade
3rd Floor
P.O. Box 838
St. Thomas, VI 00804
(809) 774-7215

Williamsburg/Brooklyn MBDC
12 Heyward St.
Brooklyn, NY 11211
(718) 522-5660

San Francisco Region (covers Alaska, American Samoa, Arizona, California, Hawaii, Idaho, Nevada, Oregon, and Washington)

MBDA Regional Director
221 Main St.
Room 1280
San Francisco, CA 94105
(415) 744-3001

MBDC Los Angeles District Office
977 North Broadway
Suite 201
Los Angeles, CA 90012
(213) 894-7157

Alaska MBDC
1577 C. St. Plaza
Suite 304
Anchorage, AK 99501
(907) 274-5400

Anaheim MBDC
6 Hutton Centre Dr.
Suite 1050
Santa Ana, CA 92707
(714) 434-0444

Bakersfield MBDC
218 South H St.
Suite 103
Bakersfield, CA 93304
(805) 837-0291

Fresno MBDC
2300 Tulace St.
Suite 210
Fresno, CA 93721
(209) 266-2766

Honolulu MBDC
1001 Bishop St.
Suite 2900
Honolulu, HI 96813
(808) 531-6232

Los Angeles 1 MBDC
1000 Wilshire Blvd.
Suite 700
Los Angeles, CA 90017
(213) 627-1717

Los Angeles 2 MBDC
601 South Fiqueroa St.
Suite 1370
Los Angeles, CA 90017
(213) 488-4949

Oxnard MBDC
451 West Fifth St.
Oxnard, CA 93030
(805) 483-1123

Phoenix MBDC
432 North 44th St.
Suite 354
Phoenix, AZ 85008
(602) 225-0740

Portland MBDC
8959 S.W. Barbur Blvd.
Suite 102
Portland, OR 97219
(503) 245-9253

Riverside MBDC
Vanir Tower
#290 North D St.
Suite 303
San Bernadino, CA 92401
(714) 386-5266

Sacramento MBDC
1779 Tribute Rd.
Suite J
Sacramento, Ca 95815
(916) 649-2551

San Diego MBDC
7777 Alvardo Rd.
Suite 310
La Mesa, CA 91941
(619) 668-6232

San Francisco/Oakland MBDC
One California St.
Suite 2100
San Francisco, CA 94111
(415) 989-2920

San Francisco/Oakland MBDC
1000 Broadway
Suite 270
Oakland, CA 94607
(510) 465-6756

San Jose MBDC
150 Almaden Blvd.
Suite 600
San Jose, CA 95150
(408) 275-9000

Seattle MBDC
155 N.E. 100th St.
Suite 401
Seattle, WA 98125
(206) 525-5617

Stockton MBDC
305 North El Dorado St.
Suite 305
Stockton, CA 95202
(209) 467-4774

Tucson MBDC
1200 North El Dorado Place
Suite F-670
Tucson, AZ 85715
(602) 721-1187

Washington, D.C. Region (covers Delaware, Maryland, Pennsylvania, Virginia, Washington, D.C., and West Virginia)

MBDA Regional Director
1255 22nd St., NW
Suite 701
Washington, DC 20036
(202) 467-0012

MBDA Philadelphia District Office
600 Arch St.
Room 10128
Philadelphia, PA 19106
(215) 597-9236

Baltimore MBDC
301 North Charles St.
Suite 92
Baltimore, MD 21201
(410) 752-7400

Newport News MBDC
6060 Jefferson Ave.
Suite 6016
Newport News, VA 23605
(804) 245-8743

Norfolk MBDC
355 Crawford Parkway
Suite 608
Portsmouth, VA 23701
(804) 399-0888

Philadelphia MBDC
125 North 8th St. 4th Floor
Philadelphia, PA 19106
(215) 629-9841

Pittsburgh MBDC
Nine Parkway Center
Suite 250
Pittsburgh, PA 15220
(412) 921-1155

Richmond MBDC
3805 Cutshaw Ave.
Suite 402
Richmond, VA 23230
(804) 355-4400

Washington MBDC
1133 15th St., NW
Suite 11220
Washington, DC 20005
(202) 785-2886

Appendix D
Additional resources

Information about financing your franchise is available from a host of sources, some of which are listed in this appendix.

International Franchise Association
1350 New York Ave.
Suite 900
Washington, DC 20005
(202) 628-8000

Women in Franchising
53 West Jackson Blvd.
Suite 756
Chicago, IL 60604
(800) 222-4943

National Association for Female Executives
127 West 24th St.
New York, NY 10011
(212) 645-0770

National Association of Small Business Investment Companies
1199 North Fairfax St.
Suite 200
Alexandria, VA 22314
(703) 683-1601

National Association of State Development Agencies
444 North Capitol St.
Suite 611
Washington, DC 20001
(202) 624-5411

National Business Incubation Association
1 President St.

Athens, OH 45701
(614) 593-4331

Fred Hale Center for Sponsored Programs
St. Louis University
DB 259
221 North Grand
St. Louis, MO 63103
(314) 533-1393

Heartland Venture Capital Network
1840 Oak Ave.
Evanston, IL 60201
(708) 864-7970

Illinois Department of Commerce and Community Affairs
Paul Gibson
Minority and Women's Program
100 West Randolph St.
Room 3-400
Chicago, IL 60601
(312) 814-7179

National Venture Capital Association
1655 North Fort Myers Dr.
Suite 700
Arlington, VA 22209
(703) 528-4370

Nebraska Business Development Center
1313 Farnam
Suite 132
Omaha, NE 68182-0248
(402) 595-2381

Appendix E

Loan agreement

LOAN AGREEMENT

THIS LOAN AGREEMENT ("Agreement") is made as of this ___ day of __ , 19__, by and among Mr. and Ms. Franchisee Company ("the Borrower") and _____ Bank ("the Lender").

RECITALS:

WHEREAS, the Lender has agreed to make a term loan to the Borrower in an amount equal to _____ Thousand Dollars ($_____) to be evidenced by a promissory note ("the Note");

WHEREAS, the parties hereto wish to set forth the terms and conditions of the loan.

NOW, THEREFORE, in consideration of the foregoing and of the agreements, covenants and conditions contained herein, and for other good and valuable consideration, the receipt and sufficiency of which is hereby acknowledged, the parties hereto agree as follows:

ARTICLE I

AMOUNT AND TERM OF LOAN

1.1   **Loan.** Subject to and upon the terms and conditions herein set forth, the Lender shall lend to the Borrower and the Borrower shall borrow from the Lender the sum of _____ Thousand Dollars ($_____).

1.2   **Note.** The Borrower's indebtedness to the Lender shall be evidenced by a promissory note (the "Note") in the form attached hereto as Exhibit 1.2.

ARTICLE II

CONDITIONS TO CLOSING

The Lender's obligations to provide the financing shall be subject to fulfillment of the following conditions prior to or at the execution of this Loan Agreement, unless otherwise waived by the Lender:

2.1   <u>Representations and Warranties True and Correct</u>. The representations and warranties made by the Borrower in Article III hereof shall be true and correct as of the execution of this Loan Agreement.

2.2   <u>Escrow</u>.   The Borrower shall have executed the Escrow Agreement, attached as Exhibit 2.2, and deposited into escrow all shares upon which the Lender shall possess a right to call.

ARTICLE III

REPRESENTATIONS AND WARRANTIES

To induce the Lender to enter into this Agreement, the Borrower represents, warrants and agrees, as of the date of this Agreement, as follows:

3.1   <u>Corporate Status: Subsidiaries</u>.   The Borrower is a corporation duly organized and validly existing under the laws of the State of _____, has the power and authority to own its properties and to carry on its business as currently conducted, and is duly qualified to do business and is in good standing in each jurisdiction in which the transaction of its business makes such qualification necessary.

3.2   <u>Borrower's Authority</u>. The Borrower has the full legal right and authority to execute, deliver and perform this Agreement. The execution, delivery and performance of this Agreement and the obligations provided for herein and in all documents required for execution hereunder (collectively "the Loan Documents") have been duly and validly authorized by all necessary corporate actions on the part of the Borrower (all of which actions are in full force and effect), and do not and will not require any consent or approval of the shareholders of the Borrower.

3.3   <u>Capital Stock</u>. The authorized capital stock of the Borrower consists of _____ thousand (_____) shares of Common Stock, with par value of one cent ($.01) per share, of which _____ (_____) shares are, as of the date of this Agreement, validly issued and outstanding, fully paid and nonassessable and held by the persons listed on Exhibit 3.3. There is no subscription, warrant, option, convertible security or other right (contingent or otherwise) to purchase or acquire any shares of any class of capital stock of the Borrower which is authorized or outstanding. The Borrower (i) has no commitment to issue any shares, warrants, options or other such rights or to distribute to holders of any class of its capital stock any evidence of indebtedness or assets, and (ii) has no obligation (contingent or otherwise) to purchase, redeem or otherwise acquire any shares of its capital stock or any interest therein or to pay any dividend or make any other distribution in respect thereof.

3.4   <u>Binding Agreement of the Borrower</u>. The Loan Documents represent the valid and legally binding obligations and agreements of the Borrower, and are enforceable in accordance with their respective terms.

3.5   <u>No Conflicting Law and Agreements</u>.   The execution, delivery and performance by the Borrower of its obligations pursuant to the Loan Documents will not violate any provisions of law, any order of any court or government instrumentality or agency, any indenture, any loan or credit agreement or any other agreement, commitment, lease, contract, deed of trust, mortgage, note or other instrument to which the Borrower is a party, or by which it or any of its property is bound, is in conflict with, will result in a breach of, or constitute (with due notice, lapse of time, or both) a default under any such indenture, agreement, commitment, lease, contract, deed of trust, mortgage, note or other instrument, or will result in the creation or imposition of any lien of any nature whatsoever upon any of the property or assets of the Borrower, or result in or require the acceleration of any indebtedness of the Borrower.

3.6   <u>Taxes</u>.   The Borrower has filed or caused to be filed all personal and corporate Federal, state and local income, excise, property and other tax returns which are required to be filed. All such returns are true and correct and the Borrower has paid or caused to be paid all taxes as shown on such returns or on any assessment received by it, to the extent that such taxes have become due, including, but not limited to, all F.I.C.A. payments and withholding taxes. To the best of the Borrower's knowledge, the amounts reserved as a liability for income and other taxes payable in the most recent financial statements of the Borrower provided to the Lender are sufficient for the payment of all unpaid Federal, state, county and local income, excise, property and other taxes, whether or not disputed, of the Borrower accrued for or applicable to the period and on the dates of such financial statements and all years and periods prior thereto and for which the Borrower may be liable in its own right or as a transferee of the assets of, or as successor to, any other person or entity.

     3.7   **Financial Condition**. The financial statements of the Borrower and other related information previously submitted to the Lender are true, complete and correct in all material respects, fairly represent the financial condition of the Borrower and the result of its operations and transactions as of the dates and for the periods of such statements and have been prepared in accordance with generally accepted accounting principles applied on a consistent basis throughout the periods involved. There are no material liabilities, direct or indirect, fixed or contingent, matured or unmatured, known or unknown, of the Borrower which are not reflected therein. There has been no material adverse change in the business, operations, prospects, assets, properties or condition (financial or otherwise) of the Borrower since the date of said financial statements.

     3.8   **Title to Properties**. The Borrower has good, valid, insurable and marketable title to all of its properties and assets (whether real or personal, tangible or intangible). All personal property in the possession of the Borrower is in good operating condition and repair and is suitable and adequate for the uses for which it is being used.

     3.9   **Litigation**. There are no actions, claims, suits or proceedings pending, or, to the knowledge of the Borrower, threatened or reasonably anticipated against or affecting the Borrower at law or in equity or before or by any governmental instrumentality or agency, commission, board, bureau, arbitrator or arbitration panel, and there is no possibility of any judgment, liability or award which may reasonably be expected to result in any material and adversarial and adverse change in the business, operations, prospects, properties or assets or condition, financial or otherwise, of the Borrower. The Borrower is not in default with respect to any judgment, order, writ, injunction, decree, rule, award or regulation of any court, governmental instrumentality or agency, commission, board, bureau, or arbitrator or arbitration panel.

3.10 No Other Defaults. The Borrower is not in default under any contract, agreement, commitment or other instrument which default would have a material adverse effect on the business, properties or condition, financial or otherwise, or in the performance of any covenants or conditions respecting any of their indebtedness hereunder. No liquidation or dissolution of the Borrower and no receivership, insolvency, bankruptcy, reorganization or other similar proceeding relative to the Borrower or its properties is pending or, to the knowledge of the Borrower, is threatened against it.

3.11 Approvals. No approval, consent or other action by any governmental instrumentality or agency or any other person or entity (which has not been received by the Borrower) is or will be necessary to permit the valid execution, delivery and performance by the Borrower under this Agreement.

ARTICLE IV

DEFAULT

4.1 Events of Default. All amounts due under a Note will become immediately due and payable at the option of the holder thereof without notice, demand, protest, notice of protest and notice of default (other than as provided for herein), presentment for payment and diligence in collection, all of which are expressly waived by the Borrower, if any one or more of the following events, each of which will be considered an Event of Default, shall occur:

(a) If default shall be made in the due and punctual payment of any installment due and owing under such Note when and as the same shall become due and payable and said default shall have continued for a period of fifteen (15) days after such payment has become due.

(b) If any statement, certificate, report, representation or warranty made or furnished by the Borrower under this Agreement shall prove to have been false or erroneous in any material respect.

(c) The occurrence of any event of default under any other financing agreement, note, lease, mortgage, security agreement or any other obligation the result of which will have a material adverse effect on the Borrower.

(d) If the Borrower shall (i) admit in writing its inability to pay its debts generally as they become due, (ii) file a petition in bankruptcy or petition to take advantage of any insolvency act, (iii) make an assignment for the benefit of its creditors, (iv) consent to the appointment of a receiver of itself or of the whole or any substantial part of its property, (v) on a petition in bankruptcy filed against it, be adjudicated as a bankrupt, (vi) file a petition or answer seeking reorganization or arrangement under the federal bankruptcy laws or any other applicable law or statute of the United States or any state there of, or (vii) distribute any of its assets upon any dissolution, wind up, liquidation or reorganization of the Borrower.

4.2   <u>Waivers by the Lender</u>.

(a) Any failure by any Lender to insist upon strict performance by the Borrower of any of the terms and provisions of any of the Loan Documents shall not be deemed to be a waiver of any of the terms and conditions thereof and such Lender shall have the right thereafter to insist upon strict performance thereof by the Borrower.

(b) The failure by any Lender to exercise the option for acceleration of maturity of such Lender's Note following any Event of Default or to exercise any other option granted hereunder shall not be deemed to constitute a waiver of any such default, but such option shall remain continuously in force.

(c) Acceleration of maturity, once claimed hereunder, may at the option of such Lender be rescinded by written acknowledgement to that effect by such Lender, but the tender and acceptance of partial payment alone shall not in any way affect or be deemed to rescind such acceleration of maturity.

(d) If any Lender shall have instituted proceedings to enforce any right under any of the Loan Documents and such proceedings shall have been discontinued or abandoned for any reason, then in every such case the Borrower and the Lender shall be restored to their former positions and the rights, remedies and powers of each Lender shall continue as if no such proceedings had been instituted.

4.3   <u>Waivers by the Borrower</u>. The Borrower hereby waives and releases:

(a) All benefits that might accrue to it under any present or future law exempting its assets or any part thereof from attachment, levy or sale on execution, or providing for any stay of execution, exemption from civil process, marshalling of assets, redemption or extension of time for payments; and

(b) Except as specifically provided herein, all notices of the Borrower's default or of a Lender's election to exercise, or any Lender's actual exercise, of any option or remedy under this Agreement or the Notes.

ARTICLE V

MISCELLANEOUS

5.1   <u>Notices</u>. All notices, demands, requests or other communications which may be or are required to be given by any party to any other party under this Agreement shall be in writing and shall be mailed by first class registered or certified mail, return receipt requested, postage prepaid, transmitted by telegram or telex, or delivered, if to the Borrower at _____, and if to Lender, at _____ _____, or to such other addresses or to the attention of such other officers as the Borrower or any Lender shall have furnished to the others in writing.

5.2   <u>Change, etc.</u>   Neither this Agreement nor any term, condition, representation, warranty, covenant or agreement contained herein may be changed, waived, discharged or terminated orally, but only by an instrument in writing signed by the party against whom such change, waiver, discharge or termination is sought.

5.3   <u>Governing Law</u>. Each of the Loan Documents shall be governed and construed in accordance with the laws of the State of _____.

5.4   Terms Binding. All of the terms of this Agreement shall apply to and be binding upon and shall inure to the benefit of the Borrower, and to each Lender, and to each of their respective successors and assigns, but the Borrower shall not have the right to assign this Agreement to any person or entity without the prior written consent of the Lender.

5.5   Invalidity of Certain Provisions. If any term or provision of this Agreement or the application thereof to any person or circumstances shall, to any extent, be invalid or unenforceable, the remainder of such term or provision or the application thereof to persons or circumstances other than those as to which it is held invalid or unenforceable shall not be affected thereby and shall be valid and enforceable to the fullest extent permitted by law.

5.6   Merger and Integration. The Loan Documents contain the entire agreement of the parties with respect to the matters covered and the transactions contemplated hereby and thereby, and no other agreement, statement or promise made by any such party, or by any employee, officer, agent or attorney of such party, which is not contained herein or therein, shall be valid or binding.

5.7   Gender, etc. Whenever used herein, the singular shall include the plural, the plural shall include the singular, and the use of the masculine, feminine or neuter gender shall include all genders.

5.8   Headings. The section and subsection headings of this Agreement are for convenience only, and shall not limit or otherwise affect any of the terms hereof.

5.9   Counterparts. To facilitate execution, this Agreement may be executed in any number of counterparts as may be required; and it shall not be necessary that the signatures of, or on behalf of, each party, or that the signatures of all persons required to bind any party, appear on each counterpart; but it shall be sufficient that the signature of, or on behalf of, each party, or that the signatures of the persons required to bind any party, appear on one or more counterparts. All counterparts shall collectively constitute a single agreement. It shall not be necessary in making proof of this Agreement to produce or account for more than a number of counterparts containing the respective signatures of, or on behalf of, all of the parties hereto.

IN WITNESS WHEREOF, each of the parties hereto have caused this Agreement to be executed, sealed and attested the day and year first above mentioned.

ATTEST: MR. & MRS. FRANCHISEE COMPANY

_____   By: _____
                                               _____

_____   By: _____
                                               _____

ATTEST: LENDER:

                                                 _____ BANK

_____   By: _____
                                      Its: _____

Appendix F

Security agreement

SECURITY AGREEMENT

THIS SECURITY AGREEMENT (the "Security Agreement") is made as of this ___ day of _____, 19__, by and between (i) _____, a Maryland corporation (hereinafter referred to as "the Borrower") and (ii) _____ Bank (the "Lender").

WITNESSETH:

RECITALS:

R-1. Pursuant to a Loan Agreement of even date herewith ("the Agreement"), the terms of which are incorporated herein by reference, Borrower has borrowed an amount equal to _____ Dollars ($_____) from the Lender as evidenced by a promissory note of even date herewith (the "Note").

R-2. Lender has required, and the Borrower has agreed, in consideration of the Lender making the loan and the benefits to be derived by the Borrower therefrom, that the Borrower grant Lender a security interest in the Borrower's assets as security for the payment of the Note.

R-3. This Security Agreement is executed in order to secure the payment of the Note and for other purposes herein set forth.

NOW, THEREFORE, in consideration of the Note, the mutual promises and covenants herein contained and other good and valuable consideration, the receipt and sufficiency of which are hereby acknowledged, the parties hereto hereby agree as follows:

1.   Incorporation of Recitals. The foregoing recitals are incorporated herein by reference to the same extent as if fully set forth herein.

2.   Definitions. As herein used:

"Account Debtor" means the Person who is obligated on an Account.

"Account" means any account as that term is defined in the Uniform Commercial Code as in effect in any jurisdiction in which any of the Collateral may at the time be located (the "U.C.C.") and includes any right of the Borrower to payment for goods sold or leased or for services rendered or money loaned which is not evidenced by an Instrument or Chattel Paper (as those terms are defined in the U.C.C.) whether or not the Account has been earned by performance.

"Chattel Paper" means any chattel paper as that term is defined in the U.C.C.

"Collateral" means (i) all of the Borrower's Accounts, General Intangibles, Chattel Paper and Instruments now existing or hereafter arising, (ii) all guarantees of the Borrower's existing and future Accounts, General Intangibles, Chattel Paper and Instruments and all other security held by the Borrower for the payment and satisfaction thereof, (iii) all of the Borrower's Inventory now owned or hereafter acquired, (iv) all of the Borrower's Equipment now owned or hereafter acquired; (v) all of the Borrower's books and records which relate to the Borrower's Accounts, General Intangibles, Chattel Paper, Instruments, Inventory and Equipment or guarantees thereof, (vi) all insurance on all the foregoing and the proceeds of that insurance and (vii) all cash and noncash Proceeds and products of all of the foregoing and the Proceeds and products of other proceeds and products.

"Equipment" means any equipment as that term is defined in the U.C.C. and shall include without limitation, all furniture, furnishings, fixtures, supplies and tangible personal property used or bought for use primarily in the Borrower's business, of every nature, presently existing or hereafter acquired or created, wherever located, additions, accessories and improvements thereto and substitutions therefor and all parts which may be attached to or which are necessary for the operation and use of such personal property or fixtures, whether or not the same shall be deemed to be affixed to real property, and all rights under or arising out of present or future contracts relating to the foregoing.

"General Intangibles" means any general intangibles as that term is defined in the U.C.C. and shall include all general intangibles of every nature, whether presently existing or hereafter acquired or created, including, without limitation, all books, correspondence, credit files, customer lists, records and other documents, computer programs, computer tapes, cards and other paper and documents in the possession or control of the Borrower and all claims, choices in action, judgments, tax refunds, patents, patent applications, trademarks, licensing agreements, royalty payments, copyrights, service names, service marks, logos, goodwill and deposit accounts.

"Instruments" means all instruments as that term is defined in the U.C.C.

"Inventory" means any inventory as that term is defined in the U.C.C. and shall include tangible personal property held for sale or lease or to be furnished under contracts of service, tangible personal property which the Borrower has so leased or furnished and raw materials, work in process and materials used, produced or consumed in the Borrower's business, and shall include tangible personal property returned to the Borrower by a purchaser or lessor thereof following the sale or lease thereof by the Borrower. All equipment, accessories and parts related, attached or added to items of Inventory or used in connection therewith and all accessions thereto shall be deemed to be part of the Inventory.

"Obligations" means all existing and future liabilities and obligations of the Borrower to the Lender, whether absolute or contingent of any nature whatsoever, now existing or hereafter incurred arising out of or relating to the Agreement or the Note, and all obligations of the Borrower to the Lender created or referred to herein.

"Person" means an individual, a corporation, a government or governmental subdivision or agency or instrumentality, a business trust, an estate, a trust, a partnership, a cooperative, an association, two or more Persons having a joint or common interest or any other legal or commercial entity.

"Proceeds" means any proceeds as that term is defined in the U.C.C. and shall include whatever is received upon the sale, exchange, collection or other disposition of Collateral or proceeds, including without limitation insurance payable by reason of loss or damage to the Collateral.

3.   Security Interest in Collateral. The Borrower hereby assigns to the Lender and grants to the Lender a lien upon and a security interest in the Collateral of the Borrower as security for the payment and performance of the Obligations. Such security interest and lien created hereby shall be subordinated as set forth in the Agreement.

4.   Security Agreement as Security for the Debentures. This Security Agreement is made to provide security for the payment of and fulfillment of all covenants and conditions of the Note, and for the fulfillment of all covenants, terms and conditions of the Agreement, this Security Agreement and any other of the Obligations, and any instrument of the Borrower evidencing and securing the Note or any other of the Obligations and for all renewals, modifications or extensions of any of the foregoing or any substitutions therefor, together with all costs, expenses, advances and liabilities, including attorneys' fees, which may be later incurred by the Lender in collection and enforcement of any of the foregoing, or any enforcement of this Security Agreement.

5.   Alteration or Amendment of Collateral.   Except as otherwise permitted herein (i) the Borrower shall not further amend or modify any documents comprising the Collateral, other than in the ordinary course of business, or waive, alter or relinquish any of its rights under the Collateral without the prior written consent of the Lender; (ii) any modification, amendment or change in the Collateral made without prior written consent of the Lender shall be a nullity; and (iii) any addendum, amendment, supplement or other modification to any of the Collateral made with the consent of the Lender shall be deemed a part of the security granted hereby.

6.   Warranties and Covenants of The Borrower. The Borrower hereby warrants and covenants as follows:

(a)   Ownership of Collateral. The Borrower is the owner of the Collateral and has (or will have when any additional collateral is acquired) the right to make this Security Agreement. The Collateral is (or will be when acquired) free and clear of all liens, security interests, claims, charges, encumbrances, taxes and assessments, except those of the Lender or those disclosed to the Lender in connection with the Note and specified in the Agreement.

(b)   Payment and Performance. The Borrower shall pay and perform all of the Obligations and liabilities secured by this Security Agreement according to its terms.

(c)   Sale of Collateral. Except as otherwise permitted herein, and except as to the sale or other disposition of the Collateral in the ordinary course of the Borrower's business, the Borrower will not sell, lease, transfer, exchange or otherwise dispose of the Collateral without the prior written consent of the Lender.

(d)   Further Assurances and Title. The Borrower will defend its title to the Collateral against all persons and will, upon request of the Lender (i) furnish further assurances of title and (ii) execute and deliver to the Lender, in form satisfactory to the Lender, any financing or continuation statement, security agreement or other document as the Lender may request in order to perfect, preserve, maintain or continue perfected the security interest created hereunder or its priority. The description in any financing statement of collateral by general classification shall not be construed to limit the Collateral assigned as described in Section 3 hereof. The Borrower will pay the costs of filing any financing, continuation or termination statements as well as any recordation or transfer tax with respect thereto and with respect to the Collateral or the security interest created by this Security Agreement.

(e)   Performance by the Lender. Upon failure by the Borrower to perform any of the acts described herein to be performed by the Borrower, the Lender, at their option and at the Borrower's sole expense, may perform any of said acts in any manner deemed proper by the Lender.

(f)   Advances Secured. All payments, costs and expenses made or incurred by or on behalf of the Lender pursuant to subparagraph (e) above or otherwise under this Security Agreement shall be deemed advanced by the Lender to the Borrower and secured by this Security Agreement. The Borrower shall pay such costs and expenses to the Lender on demand and the same shall bear interest from the date incurred or advanced until paid in full at the rate of interest then applicable to the Note.

11.   The Lender's Right in the Collateral. So long as the Obligations, or any part thereof, shall remain unpaid and this Security Agreement is in effect, upon the occurrence of any event of default under the Note, the Lender shall have all of the rights of a secured party in the Collateral.

12.   Events of Default. The Borrower shall be in default hereunder and under the Note upon the occurrence of any event of default as described in the Agreement (all or any of which are hereinafter referred to as "Events of Default").

13.   Remedies Upon Default. If an Event of Default shall occur, the Lender may, at its option, (a) declare the unpaid balance of the principal sum of the Note due together with interest accrued thereon and all other sums and indebtedness secured hereby to be immediately due and payable, and may proceed to enforce payment of the same; (b) take, retain and receive the income and profits arising from the Collateral and any other distributions of earnings, capital or otherwise, and any and all surplus thereof, and any interest whatsoever of the Borrower in the Collateral and all proceeds of the Collateral until the Obligations are paid and satisfied in full; or (c) collect, compromise or sell at public or private sale, at the option of the Lender at any time or times thereafter, without demand, advertisement or notice (other than as set forth hereinbelow or as specifically required by law), the Collateral, or any one or more or part thereof, or any substitutes therefor or additional thereto, applying the net proceeds thereof, after deduction of all costs and expenses of such collection, compromise or sale (including trustee's and attorney's fees), to the payment of the Note and/or any other of the Obligations, including interest thereon, and in case such net proceeds shall be insufficient, the Borrower shall immediately pay to the Lender the amount of such deficiency, with interest thereon at the rate then applicable to the Note from the date of the receipt, in immediately available funds of the proceeds of such collection, compromise or sale, until paid. Ten (10) days notice of the time and place of such sale shall be sent by certified or registered mail to the Borrower and the Borrower hereby waives all other notice thereof. The Borrower will sign, certify under oath and/or acknowledge an assignment of its interest in the Collateral and any and all other instruments necessary or appropriate to implement the covenants and agreements of this paragraph immediately after receipt of all such instruments. All rights conferred on the Lender hereby is in addition to those granted to the Lender by the U.C.C. and all other laws. Any notices required under the U.C.C. shall be deemed reasonable if mailed by the Lender to the parties entitled thereto at their last known addresses at least ten (10) days prior to disposition of the Collateral, or any portion thereof, and, in reference to a private sale, need state only that the Lender intend to negotiate such sale.

14.   Remedies Cumulative. Each right, power and remedy as provided for in this Security Agreement or in the Agreement and the Note or now or hereafter existing at law or in equity or by statute or otherwise shall be cumulative and concurrent and shall be in addition to every other right, power or remedy provided for in this Security Agreement or in the Agreement and the Note or now or hereafter existing at law or in equity or by statute or otherwise, and the exercise or beginning of the exercise of any one or more of such rights, powers or remedies shall not preclude the simultaneous or later exercise of any or all such other rights, powers or remedies.

15.   No Waiver. No failure or delay by the Lender to insist upon the strict performance of any term, condition, covenant or agreement of this Security Agreement or of the Agreement or the Note, or to exercise any right, power or remedy consequent upon a breach thereof, shall constitute a waiver of any such term, condition, covenant or agreement or of any such breach, or preclude the Lender from exercising any such right, power or remedy at any later time or times. No waiver of strict performance in any instance shall be deemed a waiver of such performance at any future time. By accepting payment after the due date of any amount payable under the Note or under this Security Agreement, the Lender shall be deemed to waive the right either to require prompt payment when due of all other amounts payable under the Agreement or the Note or under this Security Agreement or to declare a default for failure to effect such prompt payment of any such other amount.

16.   Termination of Security Interest. This Security Agreement and the security interest thereby created shall terminate and a termination statement shall be promptly executed and filed, upon payment in full of the Obligations secured hereby.

17.   Miscellaneous. The paragraph headings of this Security Agreement are for convenience only and shall not limit or otherwise affect any of the terms hereof. Neither this Security Agreement nor any term, condition, covenant or agreement hereof may be changed, waived, discharged or terminated orally, but only by an instrument in writing signed by the party against whom enforcement of the change, waiver, discharge or termination is sought. This Security Agreement shall be binding upon the successors and assigns of the Borrower. As used herein the singular shall include the plural as the context may require.

18.   Notices. All notices, requests, instructions or other documents required hereunder shall be deemed to have been given or made when delivered by registered mail or certified mail, return receipt requested, postage prepaid to:

If the BORROWER then:

_____

_____

_____

If the LENDER then:

_____

_____

_____

Any party may from time to time give the others notice of a change in the address to which notices are to be sent and any successors in interest.

19.   Counterparts. This Security Agreement may be executed in one or more counterpart signature pages which assembled, shall constitute a fully-executed copy hereof.

IN WITNESS WHEREOF, The Borrower and the Lender have caused this Security Agreement to be executed, sealed and delivered on the date first written above as their free acts and deeds for the uses and purposes herein stated.

THE BORROWER:

MR. AND MRS. FRANCHISEE COMPANY

ATTEST:

_____   By: _____

Secretary   _____, President

ATTEST: THE LENDER:

_____ BANK

_____   By: _____

Its: _____

Appendix G

Term promissory note

TERM PROMISSORY NOTE

$_____   _____, 19__

        FOR VALUE RECEIVED, MR. & MS. FRANCHISEE ("the Borrower"), hereby promises to pay to the order of _____ Bank ("the Lender"), the sum of _____ ($_____) with interest thereon from the date of payment for this Note at the rate set forth in Section 2.1 hereof.

        All payments to be made by the Borrower in payment of interest and principal due under this Note shall be made in the currency of the United States of America which at the time of payment shall be legal tender for the payment of public or private debts as set forth in Section 2.2 below.

        This Note is subject to the terms and conditions hereinafter set forth.

        1.   **THE NOTE.** Interest and principal on this Note shall be payable at the offices of the Borrower and mailed to the address of the Lender hereof as reflected on the Borrower's records or at such other address as the Lender may from time to time designate in writing to the Borrower.

        2.   **PAYMENTS OF PRINCIPAL AND INTEREST.**

        2.1   <u>Rate of Interest</u>. This Note shall accrue interest on the unpaid outstanding principal balance hereof at the simple rate of _____ percent (___%) per annum.

        2.2   <u>Interest Payments</u>. Interest will be payable on this Note on _____, 19__, or upon such earlier date(s) that this Note is prepaid in whole or in part.

        2.3   <u>Mandatory Principal Payments</u>. The total amount of principal advanced under this Note will be payable in full on _____, 19_.

3.   **PREPAYMENTS PRIOR TO MATURITY.** The Borrower may, at any time, without notice or penalty, prepay the Note in whole or in part. Any prepayments received with respect to the Note shall first be applied to interest then due and owing, with the remainder, if any, applied to principal.

4.   **EVENTS OF DEFAULT**

4.1   <u>Events of Default Defined</u>. The principal and interest due and owing on this Note will become immediately due and payable, at the option of the Lender, if the Borrower shall (i) admit in writing its inability to pay its debts generally as they become due, (ii) file a petition in bankruptcy or petition to take advantage of any insolvency act, (iii) make an assignment for the benefit of its creditors, (iv) consent to the appointment of a receiver of itself or of the whole or any substantial part of its property, (v) on a petition in bankruptcy filed against it, be adjudicated as a bankrupt, (vi) file a petition or answer seeking reorganization or arrangement under the federal bankruptcy laws or any other applicable law or statute of the United States of America or any state thereof, or (vii) distribute any of its assets upon any dissolution, winding up, liquidation or reorganization of the Borrower. For purposes hereof, each of the above events is hereafter referred to as an "Event of Default."

4.2   <u>Notification</u>. If an Event of Default shall occur without the Lender's knowledge, the Borrower will notify the Lender promptly in writing of the Event of Default describing it in reasonable detail, including a statement of the nature and length of existence thereof, and what action the Borrower proposes to take with respect thereto, and such written notification will be signed by one of the Borrower's officers.

5.   SUITS FOR ENFORCEMENT UPON DEFAULT. If an Event of Default shall have occurred, then and in any such event the Lender hereof may, at any time, declare the principal of and the accrued interest due under this Note to be due and payable, whereupon the same shall forthwith mature and become due and payable without demand, protest, notice of protest and notice of default, presentment for payment and diligence in collection, all of which are hereby expressly waived by the Borrower. In case any Event of Default shall occur or if this Note is not paid when due, the Lender may proceed to protect and enforce its rights hereunder by a suit in equity, action at law or other appropriate proceeding whether for the specific performance of any agreement contained herein or for an injunction against a violation of any of the terms or provisions hereof, or in aid of the exercise of any power granted hereby or by law. The Borrower covenants that if default be made in the payment of principal or interest on this Note, it will pay to the Lender, to the extent permitted under applicable law, such further reasonable amount as shall be sufficient to cover the cost and expenses of collection, including reasonable compensation to the attorneys of the Lender hereof and any court costs incurred for all services rendered in that connection. No course of dealing and no delay on the part of the Lender in exercising any rights shall operate as a waiver thereof or otherwise prejudice its rights and no consent or waiver shall extend beyond the particular case involved.

6.   NOTICES. Any request, demand, authorization, direction, notice, consent, waiver or other document permitted by this Note to be made upon, given or furnished to, or filed with the Borrower or the Lender shall be sufficient for every purpose hereunder if in writing and mailed to the Borrower, addressed to it at _____

_____ (or such subsequent address as the Borrower shall

3

advise the Lender hereof in writing) and if to the Lender at the address the Lender provides the Borrower (or at such further address as the Lender hereof shall advise the Borrower in writing). All notices required hereunder shall be deemed to have been given or made when actually delivered to or received by the party to which the notice is addressed at its respective address.

7.   MUTILATION, DESTRUCTION, LOSS, OR REISSUANCE.

7.1   <u>Mutilation</u>. This Note, if mutilated, may be surrendered and thereupon the Borrower shall execute and deliver in exchange therefor a new Note of like tenor and principal amount.

7.2   <u>Destruction, Loss, Etc.</u> If there is delivered to the Borrower (i) evidence of the destruction, loss, or theft of this Note and (ii) such security or indemnity as may be required by it to save it harmless, then, in the absence of notice to the Borrower that this Note has been acquired by a bona fide purchaser, the Borrower shall execute and deliver in lieu of such destroyed, lost or stolen Note, a new Note of like tenor and principal amount.

7.3   <u>New Note</u>. Every new Note issued in accordance with this Section in lieu of any mutilated, destroyed, lost or stolen Note shall constitute an original contractual obligation of the Borrower, whether or not the mutilated, destroyed or lost or stolen Note shall be at any time enforceable by anyone, and shall be entitled to all of the benefits of the initial Note issued.

7.4   <u>Reissuance</u>. This Note may be surrendered and thereupon the Borrower shall execute and deliver in exchange therefor, as the Lender may direct, new Notes in smaller denominations but of like tenor and in exact principal amount in the aggregate and each new Note shall constitute an original contractual obligation of the Borrower and shall be entitled to all the benefits of the initial Note issued.

      7.5   <u>Additional Sums</u>. On the issuance of any new Note under this Section, the Borrower may require of the Lender payment of a sum sufficient to cover any tax or other governmental charge that may be imposed in relation thereto and any other expenses connected therewith.

      8.   SUCCESSORS.   All of the covenants, stipulations, promises and agreements in this Note contained by or on behalf of the Borrower shall bind and inure to the benefit of its successors whether so expressed or not and also to the benefit of the Lender and its successors.

      9.   LAWS OF _____ TO GOVERN. This Note shall be deemed to be a contract made under the laws of the State of _____ and for all purposes shall be construed in accordance with the laws of such State.

      10.   TRANSFERABILITY OF NOTE. This Note is not transferable except pursuant to an effective registration statement under the Securities Act of 1933, as amended, or unless an exemption from the registration provisions of such Act is applicable.

11.   SECTIONS HEADINGS. The section headings herein are for convenience only and shall not affect the construction hereof, and the words "hereof" and "hereunder" and other words of similar import refer to this Note as a whole and not to any particular section or subdivision.

MR. & MRS. FRANCHISEE COMPANY

_____   By: _____

By: _____

Appendix H

Guaranty

GUARANTY

(1) **FOR VALUE RECEIVED**, and in consideration of the loan made by the Lender pursuant to a promissory note ("Note") issued in connection with a Loan Agreement of even date herewith ("the Agreement") by and between the Lender and the Borrower, a _____ corporation (the "Company"), the undersigned (sometimes referred to as the "Guarantor") hereby agrees to guaranty and become a surety for the full and prompt payment of all amounts due under the Note. (For purposes hereof, the indebtedness represented by the Note is hereinafter referred to as the "Guaranteed Debt").

(2) In case any Event of Default (as defined in Section 4.1 of the Loan Agreement) shall occur, such part of the Guaranteed Debt for which an Event of Default has occurred shall immediately become due and payable from the undersigned.

(3) Guarantor hereby (a) promises that in the event the Company shall at any time fail to pay the Lender when due, whether by acceleration or otherwise, any portion of the Guaranteed Debt, the undersigned, consistent with his obligations hereunder will pay such amount to the Lender forthwith, (b) agrees, (i) to any modifications of any terms or conditions of any or all of the Guaranteed Debt and/or to any renewals or extensions of time of payment or performance made by the Company, or any other guarantor if such modification does not increase the amount or frequency of payments of the Guaranteed Debt, (ii) that it shall not be necessary for the Lender to resort to legal remedies against the Company before proceeding against the Guarantor, and (iii) that no release of the Company, whether by operation of law or by any act of the Lender, with or without notice to the Guarantor shall release the undersigned; (c) waives notice of any election, acceptance, demand, protest, notice of protest and notice of

default, presentment for payment, diligence in collection, and waives, to the extent permitted by law, all benefit of valuation appraisement and all exemptions under the laws of any applicable state of the United States or under the laws of the United States and (d) agrees, if any or all of the Guaranteed Debt is not paid in accordance with the terms thereof, that Guarantor will pay, in addition to all other sums of money, all costs of collection hereunder, whether suit be brought or not, including any costs of suit and reasonable attorney's fees.

(4) This Guaranty shall continue in full force and effect until all principal and interest has been paid under the Note and all other costs and expenses arising hereunder shall have been fully paid and satisfied, including all costs of collection as above described.

(5) The Lender shall have the right, at any time and from time to time as often as it may desire, without notice to or consent of the Guarantor or any one else (said notice and consent being hereby waived) to deal with the Guaranteed Debt and each and every portion thereof and all property (the word "property" wherever used herein shall include real estate and personalty both tangible and intangible of every character wherever located) and/or liens upon property in any way securing such Guaranteed Debt or this Guaranty in such manner as the Lender in its sole discretion may deem advisable, and the Guarantor's liability hereunder shall in no way be affected or impaired by any such action or any of the following (any or all of which may be done or omitted by the Lender without notice to anyone), namely: (a) any acceptance by the Lender of any security or collateral for, or other guarantor or obligors upon, any part of the Guaranteed Debt; (b) any compromise, settlement, surrender, release, discharge, renewal, extension, alteration, exchange, sale, pledge, or other disposition of, or substitution for, or indulgence with respect to, or failure, neglect, or omission to realize upon or to enforce,

exercise, or perfect (i) any liens or right of appropriation or other rights with respect to any part of the Guaranteed Debt or any security or collateral therefor or (ii) any claims against any person or persons primarily or secondarily liable thereon; or (c) any act of commission or omission of any kind or at any time upon the part of the Lender with respect to any matter whatsoever other than the execution and delivery by the Lender to the Guarantor of an express written release or cancellation of this Guaranty. Subject to any applicable limitations of law, the Lender shall have the right to determine how, when, and what application of any payments and credits, whether derived from the Company or any other source, shall be made on the Guaranteed Debt, consistent with the terms and conditions of the Agreement or otherwise, and this Guaranty shall apply to and secure any ultimate balance that shall remain owing to the Lender.

(6) For such time as this Guaranty shall be in effect, the Guarantor shall not claim or assert any right as to any of the following: (a) to be subrogated to any position of the Lender as to any person or as to any property in any way securing the payment of the Guaranteed Debt; (b) to require the Lender to marshall any such property and/or any lien thereon; (c) to require in its capacity as a guarantor hereunder any contribution or reimbursement from the Company and/or any other party in any way liable for the payment of the Guaranteed Debt; and (d) to require the Lender to deal in any manner with any property in any way securing payment of any of the Guaranteed Debt and/or to proceed against any party or parties (including but not limited to the Company and any guarantor). The foregoing provisions of this paragraph (which are solely for the benefit of the Lender) shall not affect or modify such legal and equitable rights as the Guarantor may have after the Guaranteed Debt has been fully paid to the Lender against

3

any and all parties then and in any way liable to pay any or all of the Guaranteed Debt and/or against any and all property then securing the payment of any or all of the Guaranteed Debt, and that the Guarantor shall hold the Lender harmless from all liability to the Guarantor and/or those claims through or under the Guarantor for failure to recognize and/or failing to preserve or protect any and all legal and/or equitable rights of the Guarantor with respect to the Guaranteed Debt, the property securing the payment of the Guaranteed Debt, and/or any of the parties liable upon the Guaranteed Debt.

(7) Except as otherwise provided in the Agreement, the Lender may, without notice to anyone, sell, assign or otherwise transfer the Note, or any part thereof, or grant participation therein, and in any such event each and every immediate or remote assignee or holder of, or participant in, all or any part of the Note shall have the right to enforce this Guaranty, by suit or otherwise, for its benefit, as fully as if herein by name specifically given such right; but the Lender shall have an unimpaired right, prior and superior to that of any such assignee, holder, or participant, to enforce this Guaranty for the benefit of the Lender, as to any part of the Guaranteed Debt retained by the Lender.

(8) No postponement or delay on the part of the Lender in the enforcement of any right hereunder shall constitute a waiver of such right, and all rights of the Lender hereunder shall be cumulative and not alternative and shall be in addition to any other rights granted the Lender in any other agreement or by law.

(9) The provisions hereof shall be binding upon the undersigned, his heirs, executors, administrators, legal representatives, successors and assigns.

(10) If any term or provision hereof shall be, or shall be declared to be, invalid, illegal or unenforceable in any respect, such invalid, illegal or unenforceable provision shall be and become absolutely null and void and of no force and effect as though such term or provision were never included herein, but all other covenants, terms, conditions, and provisions hereof shall nevertheless continue to be valid and enforceable and this Guaranty shall be so construed.

(11) This Guaranty shall be construed according to the laws of the State of _____.

WITNESS the due execution and sealing hereof by the Guarantor with the intent of being legally bound as of the ___ day of _____, 19___.

WITNESS: GUARANTOR:

_____   _____

                                         _____

Glossary

accounts receivable: Money owed to a business for goods or services sold on open account.

amortization: A schedule of equal monthly payments that will pay the loan in full over a given period of time. Payments may include level principal payments *plus* interest (total payments will usually decline each month), or equal monthly payments of principal *and* interest (total payments will stay the same for the full term of the loan). The loan term may run for the full amortization period or may be shorter (a 5-year term with a 15-year amortization) with a large "balloon" payment at maturity for the unpaid balance of the loan.

balloon: A feature of a loan such that final payment is substantially larger than previous payments. This is used particularly where refinancing is expected or where some future event is expected to increase cash flow.

business plan: A document that describes in detail the company's history, current status, and future direction. It should include all the historical financials, such as the projected balance sheet, profit and loss statement, a statement of cash flow, and a personal financial statement.

cash flow lending: A loan in which the bank focuses on the borrower's cash flow as the means to repay the debt.

co-borrower: An additional person who is primarily liable for payment of a debt.

collateral: Assets pledged by the borrower to the lender until the debt is repaid. If the borrower defaults, the lender may seize such assets and sell them to pay the loan.

demand loan: A loan in which the bank may demand repayment at any time.

guarantee: A promise to pay a debt or perform an obligation if the person primarily liable defaults.

interest: The cost of using money, expressed as a rate per period of time (usually 1 year, in which case it is called an annual rate of interest).

inventory: Goods held for sale or lease (including raw materials, work in progress, and finished goods), and goods used and consumed in the business.

lien: A creditor's claim against property; for example, mortgages and security interests are liens.

loan value: The amount a lender is willing to lend against collateral. For example, at 50 percent loan value, property worth $100,000 has a loan value of $50,000.

lock box: A cash management system whereby a company's customers send payments to a post office box near the company's bank. The bank collects checks from the lock box—sometimes several times a day—and deposits them into the firm's account. The bank then notifies the company's cash manager of the deposit.

mortgage: A lien, usually against real estate.

principal: The face amount of a debt instrument on which interest is owed or earned.

notice and cure provision: A provision entitling the borrower to notice of defaults by the borrower and an opportunity to cure such defaults before the lender exercises its remedies.

revolving loan: A loan in which the borrower may borrow up to a specified maximum amount over a period of time. When the borrower repays all or part of the loan, he or she may reborrow again up to the maximum amount during the period of time. Often, the borrower is required to pay the balance down periodically. This is particularly useful when the borrower's cash flow needs vary seasonally.

secured debt: A debt backed by a pledge of collateral.

security interest: A creditor's lien against personal property such as inventory, equipment, and accounts receivable.

term loan: A loan for a specified period of time (as opposed to a demand loan) that does not have a revolving feature. This usually refers to a commercial secured loan with an intermediate to long term (typically 2 to 10 years), and it sometimes has a balloon feature.

Index

About the Authors

MEG WHITTEMORE is associate editor of *Nation's Business* magazine, published by the U.S. Chamber of Commerce, where she covers the latest developments in franchising and small store retailing. She is a leading authority on franchising. She was formerly communications director for the International Franchise Association and provided marketing counsel to the franchise community.

ANDREW SHERMAN is a Washington-based attorney with Silver, Freedman & Taff, and a national authority on the legal and strategic issues affecting franchises and small businesses. A contributor to *Nation's Business* magazine, he is the author of *One Step Ahead: The Legal Aspects of Business Growth, Franchising and Licensing: Two Ways to Build Your Business,* and managing editor of *The Franchising Management Handbook.*

RIPLEY HOTCH writes for *Nation's Business* magazine, is an authority on franchising issues, and author of *How to Start a Business and Succeed* and *How to Start and Run Your Own Bed & Breakfast Inn.*